Concepts of Normality

by the same author

Friendships
The Aspie Way
Wendy Lawson
Foreword by Emma Wall
ISBN 978 1 84310 427 8

Sex, Sexuality and the Autism Spectrum
Wendy Lawson
Foreword by Glenys Jones
ISBN 978 1 84310 284 7

Build Your Own Life
A Self-Help Guide for Individuals with Asperger Syndrome
Wendy Lawson
Foreword by Dr Dinah Murray
ISBN 978 1 84310 114 7

Understanding and Working with the Spectrum of Autism
An Insider's View
Wendy Lawson
ISBN 978 1 85302 971 4

Life Behind Glass
A Personal Account of Autism Spectrum Disorder
Wendy Lawson
Foreword by Patricia Howlin
ISBN 978 1 85302 911 0

ASPoetry
Illustrated Poems from an Aspie Life
Wendy Lawson
Illustrated by Alice Blaes Calder
ISBN 978 1 84310 418 6

Concepts of Normality
The Autistic and Typical Spectrum

Wendy Lawson

Forewords by Lucy Clark and
Petra and Magnus Björne

Jessica Kingsley Publishers
London and Philadelphia

First published in 2008
by Jessica Kingsley Publishers
116 Pentonville Road
London N1 9JB, UK
and
400 Market Street, Suite 400
Philadelphia, PA 19106, USA

www.jkp.com

Library of Congress Cataloging in Publication Data

Lawson, Wendy, 1952-

Concepts of normality : the autistic and typical spectrum / Wendy Lawson ; foreword by Lucy Clark.

p. cm.

Includes bibliographical references.

ISBN 978-1-84310-604-3 (pb : alk. paper) 1. Autism—Social aspects. 2. Individuality. 3. Conformity. I. Title.

RC553.A88L388 2008

616.85'882—dc22

2008004750

British Library Cataloguing in Publication Data

A CIP catalogue record for this book is available from the British Library

ISBN 978 1 84310 604 3

Printed and bound in Great Britain by
Athenaeum Press, Gateshead, Tyne and Wear

Contents

Acknowledgements

Over the many years of my 'growing up' so many different individuals have steered me towards a life of self-acceptance and positive self-esteem. They taught me that normality is multi-sided and multi-faceted. It incorporates all the variety and variation that enables a rainbow to dazzle us with her colours through the sun rays and the rain drops. To all of those individuals I owe a debt of gratitude.

In particular, to my partner Beatrice, who taught me that the human body with all its imperfections is beautiful, I say 'Thank you'.

To my current friends and family, who continue to play such a huge role in my life enabling me to stay focused and on track. To my co-contributors of this book, sharing a common vision and fight gives us each such strength. I've benefited from your strength and I know others will too. To Sarah whose feedback and editing support means so much. To Dinah, David and Judy, without whose love and encouragement the world would be a very much darker place, thank you.

Foreword

In writing the foreword to this important book, I am delighted to be able to contribute toward Wendy's call to power to those who experience the constraints of the current concept of 'normality'. This book asks that we all challenge and reconsider our limitations, work together to expand the boundaries of 'normal diversity' and help to break down visible and invisible barriers between autistic people and the rest of the population. We all have a personal responsibility to answer that call.

The individual (or medical) model of disability remains all too evident in much of the current literature on autism and it inevitably and invariably informs the way that support services are constructed for autistic people. This model works from an assumption that people are disabled by their personal deficits, and if those deficits can be corrected or minimized, usually by professional intervention, the individual will be more able to exist in 'normal' society, living side by side with 'normal' people. With this model in place, efforts are ploughed into training the autistic person to masquerade as 'normal', to be indistinguishable from those without an autism diagnosis – to speak, make eye contact, stand and sit still, stop flapping their hands or using them to cover their ears, to share popular culture interests and to process and remember complex communicative content. Autistic people have been over-medicated, inappropriately restrained, ignored, abused and undervalued throughout history. This must stop. We all tend unquestioningly to value professional opinion over our own, and we are assumed to be grateful for help and expected to be compliant with those who choose to help us; we can too easily become passive recipients of services and interventions offered in lieu of empowerment, rights, control and individualism.

As Wendy articulates from both a personal and political perspective in this book – the individual model damages people. It hurts their sense of self, their sense of personal power; it takes away their rights and their control; it trespasses into their relationships with their peers and affects their self-esteem; and it supports the use of everyday language that places people in the 'passive' or 'recipient' role. However, everybody needs help, support, love and care; we all need other people to do things with us, and sometimes for us, because we don't always know how, or because we can't physically manage it on our own.

We therefore need to redefine our concept of 'normality' and to embrace one which includes and accepts difference; we need to celebrate diff-ability in learning style and speed, interests, communication style, dress sense and personal choice. We need to replace the structures and the language that highlight and perpetuate a position of powerlessness for autistic people.

The social model locates the responsibility for disability in the way that society is structured. This model separates the personal from the socio-political. It affirms that although we cannot (and should not) change the way that we and other people are as individuals, we can change the way that support is provided and services are structured.

We can change the way that people have access to health services, education and employment, and we can change the language that we use to talk about and address each other and our needs. We all have a responsibility to help to break down the barriers that exclude people, whether they are physical barriers (stairs, the way that public spaces are arranged), communication barriers (language, the provision of information) or attitudinal barriers (prejudice, disgust, fear, exclusivity), so that people can better and more autonomously exercise their right to choose how to live their lives.

In all too many ways, societal and attitudinal barriers exclude people who do not fit into what has habitually been the accepted concept of 'normality'. As this book demonstrates, the current concept is unacceptable because it disables and excludes autistic people. Social and attitudinal barriers support this antiquated concept of 'normality' and perpetuate its existence and acceptance.

This book explores how we could and should redefine the normality concept, moving the barriers, sometimes removing them, in order that people on the autistic and typical spectrums can better live side by side, engaging in reciprocal and supportive relationships, and each claiming their right to full participation in a lifestyle of their choosing.

Lucy Clark
Director of People and Culture
Homes Caring for Autism Ltd

Foreword

At the end of the 1960s a paper was published that led to an international debate about the conditions under which people with disabilities were living. The title of the paper was: 'The Normalization Principle and its Human Management Implications'. The author, Bengt Nirje, was then working as a representative for the Swedish Association for Retarded Children, a parental organization. The paper originated in the fact that many persons with intellectual disabilities were at the time living in enormous institutions in almost inhuman circumstances.

Nirje demanded normalization. The idea was not to normalize the individual person by adapting him or her to behave according to the norms of society. The idea was rather to normalize the conditions under which people with intellectual and other disabilities were living and how they were being met. The basic tenet was that people with disabilities had the right to live and to be treated like others, like human beings. That is, to be allowed to participate in large and small decisions concerning their own lives, by living in a society normally accessible to them. Nirje argued that those with an intellectual disability had the same rights and responsibilities as did other citizens, and that they should be allowed to assume and exert those rights and responsibilities, just as anyone else.

Although almost 40 years have passed since the publication of Nirje's paper, there is still much to be done to reach the proposed ideals. The huge institutions are history, at least in Sweden, but people with disabilities of any kind, including autism, are in reality seldom given the chance to assume the same civil rights granted other citizens. The possibility to decide in questions concerning oneself is still limited for all too many. Furthermore, adapting the individual to the norms prevalent in society is still discussed.

It is time that we abandon this outdated way of viewing people with disabilities. Equal rights for all citizens should be a matter of course. One important step in reaching this is to really discuss what we mean when we talk about normal, normality and normalization. Otherwise an unreflected demand for normal behaviour will exclude those unable to conform to the requirements. Current research involving people living on the autism spectrum shows that people with autism develop in a different way. Being different and thinking along different lines may be a very normal outcome of a different developmental trajectory. It by no means implies that the person is of less worth or is abnormal, not even when the difference leads to a need for support. Being different should not be imbued with a negative value.

In this book, Wendy argues, and we could not agree more, that normality is a much more complex concept than we initially tend to realize. Trying to identify groups in society that are more normal than others is a rather meaningless task. Normality cuts through all kinds of groups, and who is normal or not changes from context to context. We often are, but need not really be, afraid of what we perceive as being not normal. Wendy eloquently and intelligently shows the reader that openness towards and curiosity in different abilities can be highly rewarding for all parties involved!

Petra Björne, PhD Cognitive Science
Magnus Björne, Pedagogical Consultant

Introduction

Over the years, understanding the concept of 'normality' has become very important to me. Hearing a significant other saying about me 'she was never normal' only contributed to the desire to explore what being normal really means. What I have come to appreciate is the sheer diversity and variation that naturally exists side by side in a whole range of normal. The reason for writing this book, therefore, is to explain and explore current understandings of normal in ways that help demystify and qualify normal, which might allow us all access to the full range of human experience. For those of us with autism, understanding typical descriptions of normal can be a huge task. For those of us without autism, the perception of the term *normal* can lead to unrealistic expectations of self and of others.

Currently the debate about 'what is normal' is causing some heated exchange; this is not new. In particular the debate concerning autism, disability, neuro-diversity and typicality poses some ongoing challenges. Disability presents itself in a variety of ways, and for most of us living with disability, who we are is normal for us. For many people on the autism spectrum, which is certainly very disabling in a world that does not accept, value or accommodate 'difference', being handicapped is an everyday reality. This text argues for the right to exist as oneself, with or without disability; this should be part of 'the norm'. It does not argue for the right to exist in order to upset, displace, disrespect or disenfranchise another. Having a respectful understanding of one another should include accessibility to appropriate resources, support, safe places and sincere appreciation of difference. Anything less is not acceptable.

In our understanding of normal, the following will need to be considered:

- the world's societal norms concerning human expectation might be different
- the ways in which various societies perpetuate tradition and gender roles
- societal understanding of Western values in particular associated with 'having value'
- traditions born from 'the medical model' compared to social models of any given society
- the individual and community 'mind' values that are seen as assets
- how concepts are formed and what impact they have upon the forming of the concept 'normal'
- whether normalizing 'difference' could enhance existing schemas to accommodate disability and welcome it as an enrichment of normal rather than seeing it as entrapment
- the place of life traps in their nurturing of existing societal schemas that hinder the wider accommodation of difference as a legitimate part of normal and, therefore, maintain the status quo.

To understand normal and value its implications for life, learning and good practice, one needs to explore the relationships outlined above and their positions within our societal hierarchies. This book seeks to explain some of these concepts surrounding typical views of autism and many of the traditional views of perceived normality. By exploring terms concerning traditional views of normal and the developing, now typical, concept of the autism spectrum, a picture is drawn of how and why these views developed. It is hoped that a journey that maps these concepts and seeks to open up this territory will mean accessibility for individuals who might grow to feel more at home with who they are and with what it means to be normal for them. That means most of us!

First, the book briefly outlines some ideas behind Western societal current thinking and beliefs that have led to the building of a society that hungers for exclusivity, but comes up wanting. Second, it will describe, in practical terms, what a wider concept of normal means and how to access it. Whether it's in normal social interaction, normal kinds of friendships, normal feelings, normal thoughts, normal desires or any other aspects of normality, we all experience these in a variety of ways in everyday situations.

Being exclusive means failing to be inclusive, and yet we see 'exclusive' propagated all around us. So the need to fit in and not be different is counterbalanced with the need to be an individual. There are so many examples of this in everyday life. Whether it's in aiming to have some unique model of motor car, a piece of furniture, an outfit no one else has or a monopoly over some supermarket chain. Why do we have designer jeans and fashion that begs a size 6 (UK10) when most women are a size 10 (UK14)? Is this just competition to outdo one another or is it more sinister? I think the latter!

In Chapter 7 my colleague and friend Dinah Murray shows how particular behaviours are common and normally found in individuals on both the typical and autistic spectrums. Dinah does this by illustrating and highlighting the typical behaviours (emotions) used by both populations, but also with respect to how each may respond to the other. In Chapter 9 Estée Klar-Wolfond, director of The Autism Acceptance Project, also a colleague and friend, takes us on a journey demonstrating the reality of a world where autistic individuals may or may not be valued. One where societal concepts of normal clothed in inclusive language can offer positive pictures of a very real future for those of us with autism. Estée's ideas could be a reality in a society that welcomes difference as a usual part of normal.

Ultimately this book suggests we take back control over a wider societal understanding of normal, enabling us to create a more inclusive schema or way of thinking. Society as a whole can be thought of as consisting of a vast system of overlapping communities of interest, each made up of individuals with their own sets of interests. Every interest is what it is as a result of a learning history during which relevant facts have informed it. Schemata can therefore be thought of as the forms of interests. With this understanding in mind, it is easier to comprehend how humans interact with one another and why we are so controlled by what we think others are thinking of or wanting from us.

Some definitions of *normal*

Whether defined by a dictionary or online by Wikipedia the definition of normal has many sides and aspects to it that range from behaviour (e.g. moral and sexual behaviours) to institutions, such as marriage and social convention. It suggests normal refers to 'a lack of significant deviation from the average'. Wikipedia goes on to say 'the phrase "not normal" is often applied in a negative sense (asserting that someone or some situation is improper, sick, etc.)'. Apparently the word comes from the Latin *normalis* and implies that the most common behaviour in a society is considered normal. Of course, there are many sub-groups in any given society where 'the group' sets out the rules for what is usual, typical or normal for that group. If one is a collector of coins, stamps, fine china, vintage cars or superhero magazines, one could argue that this is normal for the individual collector or the 'special interest' group they belong to, whilst it mightn't be normal for another individual who doesn't have that interest or occupation. So, in every respect the idea of normal must always be implicitly relative to a point of view or interest.

The other way of looking at this is to think of what is most commonly occurring in any mainstream situation. This means that the ordinary or usual practice for the majority could be considered 'normal'. Of course, there are all sorts of difficulties with this definition. History has shown there have been times when whole societies were involved in destructive and abominable practices that have seen entire populations of people wiped from the face of the earth. Many of these practices were carried out in the name of normal.

When it comes to fashionable expectation and body beautiful the advertising media in Western society play a large role in shaping what is considered normal. For example, in 2008 many young girls feel unhappy with their bodies because theirs are not like those they read about in the glossy magazines. For these young girls what is promoted as beautiful and desirable is converted in their minds to normal and something they 'must have' to be considered acceptable. It's not unusual for the media to play a role in promoting what any given society comes to believe about normal for its population. However, the media are not often held accountable for the irresponsible promotion of wrong beliefs, attitudes and misconceptions.

So, if normal is governed by societal rules, prohibitions, changing fashions, fads, political ambitions and the fickleness of human nature, how can we know what is truly normal or what is truly 'right'? How would it be if we rephrased this question and asked ourselves: 'What makes something abnormal or "wrong"?' This book aims to answer this question and point to ways that enable one to feel comfortable inside one's own skin.

Definition of some other terms

Although it might become apparent just what the various terms used in this book will mean, I am also giving some brief definition in this introduction.

With the idea of 'people first' it has become common to think of individuals with autism rather than of autistic individuals. Whereas I completely agree with this sentiment, many individuals I know (including myself) feel that their autism isn't some added-on appendage but is who they are. Out of respect for them and without wishing to upset others, wherever I am writing in this text, I will use the term *autistic individuals*. I will also refer to AS (autism spectrum), TS (typical spectrum) and AD (Asperger's disorder) as ways of differentiating either learning styles or specific populations. However, because the autism spectrum covers a wide experience of autism the term AS also refers to a variety of labels that exist as part of the autism continuum. Some of those individual labels are explained later on in the text.

ASD (autism spectrum disorder) is another common term used to refer to the autism spectrum. When I use ASD I am referring to autism spectrum diff-ability or to be differently abled. This does not take away from the difficulties or suggest those of us with ASD don't need support, rather it aims to do the opposite. It is precisely because of our diff-ability, and all that means, that autism should be high on the agenda for recognition as a particular way of being. For some individuals autism is one of the ways they experience the world. They may also be living as individuals influenced by intellectual disability, attention deficits, epilepsy, dyspraxia, dyslexia and others. Therefore, some individuals will have multi-complex needs that need specialized support. However, this support should be normal for them enabling them to live as anyone else might. For more on these concepts see Murray, Lesser and Lawson (2005).

Polytropism is a term used to describe a processing resource that includes divided attention governed by a diverse and diffuse interest system (Murray 1992). It is associated with the TS and requires a brain configuration that allows for multi-sensory practice informing a perception action loop (Björne 2007; Lawson 2001; Murray, Lesser and Lawson 2005). *Monotropism* is a term used to describe a processing resource including single attention governed by a tight system of highly focused interests that take precedence over everything else. It requires a brain configured to work with a single sense or a less integrated sensory system allowing only a single focus of interest at any one time. I believe that there are polytropic and monotropic continuums and that we each move along such a continuum in particular ways throughout our lives. For more on these concepts see Murray, Lesser and Lawson (2005).

Language is a term commonly used to define the spoken word. Language comes in many guises, however, and, when used to define concepts of communication, may be presented in other formats, not just verbal. Language may mean signing, using visual supports, projected speech from typed scripts via machines, non-verbal body language, and so on. In Chapter 7 Dinah Murray suggests we look at Amanda Baggs' video entitled 'In My Language' for a broader understanding of language.

Others and the singular *Other* are words used in the text, particularly in Chapter 7, to mean members of the typical population. In writing about how Others typically encounter autism a description is given that allows one to comprehend and identify behaviours typically found in both populations.

I hope all other terms will be self-explanatory. I trust this book will be a good read for you. I also hope it challenges and encourages you. Most of all, I hope it contributes to societal images of normal making a positive difference in the lives of individuals for many generations to come.

CHAPTER 1

Developing Images and Concepts of Normality

Changing expectations: Normal yesterday may not be normal today

I was born only seven years after the Second World War ended. Much of my parents' concern for my siblings and me was that we should have a better and easier life than the one they had experienced during years of depression, hardship and war. They were determined for my brother to access education and for my sisters and me to have a secure home life. They didn't expect, however, that my sisters would study at university or have careers, as much as they expected they would leave school at 15, work for a few years, then marry and have children.

It was not so usual, in those days, for women to go to university or to enter careers usually reserved for men. However, the war years had seen women take over jobs that were not considered typical or normal for women to do. This was out of necessity because the men were away at war. So, for a number of years women drove heavy vehicles, and worked as engineers, labourers, and so on. This had a knock-on effect when the war ended because the men came home and expected to get their jobs back and their women to return to more domestic pursuits. But for some of those women it had become normal to work in what was once considered a male occupation. Some of them did not want to return to domestic duties, and they fought to keep their jobs.

Although this was a turbulent time and the fight for equality between the sexes still exists, those years happened and the clock could not be turned back. We can see, therefore, that the experiences of our fathers and mothers shape the foundations of normal for future generations.

Psychology, meaning and wellbeing

In many ways 20th-century psychology has much to account for in our current understanding of normal. Psychology seeks to explain much of the behaviour we humans adopt. However, in doing so it also suggests there is normal psychology and abnormal psychology. In some ways this is unfortunate terminology because it fails to locate normal and/or abnormal in individual human experience but rather takes the typical or usual in the majority and says that is normal. Also trying to understand self and others in terms of psychology is difficult because there are so many branches to explore.

Whether you are a Freudian supporter, a believer in the behaviourist theory of learnt responses, a follower of cognitive approaches or someone who views each life as one that is 'relative' and controlled by environmental factors, you will probably be living subject to a whole set of beliefs you hardly knew were there. Psychology is so embedded within our Western society that its influences are no longer separate from one's own thinking and ideology. It is, therefore, a challenge to tease out these beliefs and question them. However, I hope to give enough basic and foundational snippets of relevant information to make this possible.

Developmental psychology (lifespan psychology) considers how and why our psychological characteristics change over time. It suggests that personality, relationships, cognition and biology all play a part in this process (Cooper and Roth 2002). This chapter's focus is primarily upon things generally considered normal in the area of relationships, personality and cognition. It considers these in relation to their influence upon lifespan development. It shows how normal in one generation isn't always experienced as normal in another.

To date, developmental psychology has tended to focus mainly upon childhood development. Therefore, in the past, it has failed to see the value of adult experiences upon the lifespan (Cooper and Roth 2002). Although it is quite obvious that lifespan development must include adult experiences, too often these are not considered.

Maybe this is because as adults we are each considered grown up and the notion of constant change is neglected. For most of us, though, the connections that form and change our ideas are not only forged between adult outcomes from childhood experiences, but also adult outcomes from adult experiences.

Developmental psychology appears to take much of its rationale from a variety of overlapping psychological fields or perspectives. It suggests that lifespan development is influenced by an array of activities. Within this eclectic approach there is room for evolutionary psychology, biological psychology, psychodynamic, psychometric, social and cognitive perspectives (Cooper and Roth 2002).

When individuals share their stories with one another it becomes clear just how much of an impact psychological perspectives and their influences have over our lives. For example, even in the words we use to describe our experiences, we are creating pictures of 'self' and of 'other' through sets of interests or schemes. We may use words such as 'usually', 'typically', 'normally', 'yours', 'mine', and so on. These words build pictures that are then translated cognitively and become psychological domains or 'givens'.

Experiences like depression and anxiety may have their roots in the environment, as well as in one's biology, according to evolutionary psychology. For example, many of our ancestors during cave-dwelling times chose to live where they could see some distance from home. They did this because they needed to be able to spot if their enemies were approaching, as well as to see if deer were nearby for food. Their need to be able to defend and feed themselves was paramount to their sense of wellbeing. So, if they couldn't see way off to the distance or if their ability to hunt for food was inhibited, they moved on to other places that suited their needs better. However, if this was not possible to do, adapting to the environment sometimes became too stressful and in-house fighting caused whole families to die out (Hockett and Ascher 1992).

I know what a difference it has made to how I feel about life when I can stand on top of a hill and look off into the distance. I also know how gloomy life can feel when one feels 'stuck' or cornered without a hope of finding a way out. Some of our Western terminology with regard to wellbeing may have its origin in evolutionary psychology. For example, 'I'm feeling on top of things' or 'I'm feeling down in the dumps'.

If one's sense of wellbeing or of belief that one's destiny is in one's control is removed, or if one feels disabled by means of physical, social or attitudinal barriers within society, then 'normal' expectations may seem out of reach too. Without a sense of value, meaning or wellbeing, the richness of life remains elusive. We may not live in caves very much these days, but we each still need to find meaning for our lives to make sense. This is one reason we need to have interests and why we engage in sharing the interests of others. It could be argued that most relationships are based around sets of interests.

Personality is a definite factor that influences lifespan development. However, one must ask, what shapes personality? Has there been a disposition to certain traits all of our lives, or have these changed over time? The research seems to suggest that personality is pretty stable over time, but that it might change in any particular direction by as much as 5 per cent (Burger 1993). It would seem that, although the personality you and I have is influenced to a great extent by genetics, it is also influenced by the environment (social, emotional and physical), as well as by 'thoughts that lie outside our immediate awareness' (Burger 1993, p.539).

What role does education play in the construct of what we come to believe about normal? Is it only formal education that should be considered? Of course it isn't. Education is also an interaction of learning, interests and experiences shared through stories passed on to us by family, friends and the media. Some of us are concerned that the media has greater influence over what we come to believe about ourselves than do the voices of the relationships we share with others.

We may be fortunate to have grown up in loving families where our sense of worth has been fostered appropriately. We may have accessed a full and long period of formal education. Does this mean that we will make better decisions and earn higher salaries than an individual who didn't spend much time in formal education and who didn't develop a positive sense of self? Probably. What are the influences on our cognitive development, though, and is it all the same anyway? Most of us would realize that we each have differing learning styles, and that the emotional as well as physical environments we grow up in play a huge role in the development of self-esteem. Some people learn well from life experiences and see the hurdles faced as opportunities and ways to problem-solve in the future. Others see the difficulties only as obstacles rather than opportunities. Some people need structure and rely upon routine and order to get through the day. What is the normal way you and I learn? It's probably different for each of us. But being different does not make one learning style superior to another so much as it makes for variety and furthers the development of communities of interests.

So, how have life experiences influenced societal life and is it the same for our children? What governs our:

- choice of spouse
- choice of career
- beliefs about rights
- expectations for our own children?

Research shows us that we each are more drawn to what is familiar and comfortable. We are more likely to choose a partner that represents Mr or Mrs Average than we are someone outside of that domain. Difference can cause conflict, so we tend to avoid it. But sometimes conflict is healthy, and dealing with conflict and solving problems tends to make us more confident and capable. It's the fuel of courage and consistency.

I noticed when talking to several of my married friends that many couples speak about how important it is to have their independence from one another. The fact that they don't see themselves as having 'a shared identity' demonstrates this. Maybe the need to learn to depend upon oneself and not need someone else, a type of 'self-reliance', was formed during the war years and has laid a foundation for strong independence? However this has come about, it has changed over time. Not so long ago it was normal or usual for whole families to work together and interdependence was necessary for survival. These days, however, being independent and not needing others in one's life is often seen as honourable and noble. This belief has been exploited further by various business opportunities. There are many who see an interest for themselves in making money out of promoting the rights of individuals, for example the right to have material goods. This policy, developed further through advertising and using words to build concepts that appeal to ego, continues to drive 21st-century beliefs about individual rights.

The right to education, the right to good health, the right to have one's needs met and one's appetite satisfied...not all of this is bad, but, unfortunately, one's right to these things has been propelling a societal mindset that is promoting individual rights over human rights. In developing a concept of normal based upon one particular set of norms, diversity and difference as part and parcel of everyday normal or typical life is being lost rather than being cultivated. It seems it is not in the interest of big business to resource and support difference so much as it is to promote expensive and unreachable goals that keep us all reaching for the moon!

With regard to the expectations many of us have for our children, perhaps we have been led to believe, mostly by advertising material promoted via various media, that to have a good life one must be physically handsome, well educated, earn lots of money and not be disabled by personal difficulties. This serves the corporate interest rather than the human interest and, sadly, has captured the minds of millions.

So, even though the lifespan perspective suggests we are all an ongoing product of our social, emotional and physical environments, it has failed to promote inclusion of difference. Maslow would argue that we each display a hierarchy of needs that dictate our goals (Peterson 1989). But these goals have been exploited as 'must haves' in Western society and are now intricately woven through societal schemata and embedded in our psyche.

However, it isn't just lifespan or developmental psychology suggesting we are all only a product of nature and nurture. Social psychology says that social relationships dictate the way we relate; thus, if we are not given to being sociable, then we must be faulty and not normal.

This belief can lead us to being guarded with friends or individuals we like because we want to impress them. Theatrical imagination (the type of imagination requiring an audience), very much a part of typical development, predisposes society towards the building of an interest system that is based upon deception. Why let anyone really see who you really are and the difficulties you really face when it might mean exposure to the reality that you don't always succeed and are not always winning? Failure isn't in the interest of a society and business ethic that views success as the only valid goal.

With strangers, however, we are perhaps more open because we don't have to relate to them in any ongoing manner. Maybe we are more real when we don't feel the need to impress. But, if fake is promoted as the norm, then being real and being needy is seen as not normal.

When it comes to expectations of what is normal with regard to attachment, work ethic, marriage, gender roles, family, and so on, the literature suggests many childhood influences upon adult outcomes (Peterson 1989). But why do we choose to believe there is only one way to be that is normal? It's as if we have been hoodwinked by our own short-sightedness and have got caught up in an expectation of normal.

I have not experienced war first hand. I did, however, know poverty, frequent relocation, illness and disability. This would influence how I see and experience the things I consider normal for me. Truth, as a construct, is relative and is formed from a number of beliefs coloured by our own experiences, for example age, gender, societal disposition, education, belief systems and, of course, for many, the desire to fit in and belong. Maybe it is this last one that offers the heaviest weight for so many?

Wouldn't it be wonderful if society could open its arms to each of us and give us the message that we are welcome, just the way we are? I love the story of Mumble from the film *Happy Feet*.

The penguin Mumble was born a little later than most, developed more slowly and had a heart song that was not a verbal song, but a dance. Within Mumble's penguin population, no other penguin danced like him. To find others of like mind, Mumble had to leave his family and all he had known. He travelled far and wide and experienced incredible hardship that nearly claimed his life. It was only because he found an eye and an ear in the shape of a little girl, not yet programmed to see only typical normality, that his life was saved. The little girl saw and heard Mumble in a way that adults had missed. She was able to encourage her family to see him too and, eventually, the world listened to Mumble and took up his vision. It was this openness to seeing the bigger picture and to working towards changing a developing scheme (that was pushing a population of penguins towards extinction) that saved the entire situation, including Mumble.

We need more Mumbles, more Mumble acceptance and more Mumble action if we are to save human integrity and develop a wider, more inclusive schema of normal.

As human beings we each grow up in families that may have either a positive or negative impact upon us as developing adults. As adults we each contribute to the belief systems of our particular family, by perpetuating and nurturing those beliefs. According to Young and Klosko (1994), the things we believe about ourselves and about others can become life traps, particularly if they keep us prisoners to negative and destructive outcomes. Young and Klosko argue that life traps are behind the various personality disorders that plague so many of us. It is suggested, however, that such beliefs are not only associated with negative outcomes but also heavily integrated into the art of 'being normal'. In other words, being normal for many means let's look at ways to swap neuroses!

Cognitive theory suggests that we each are the outcome of our thinking. It's as we change our negative thinking to that of a more positive image, our emotional responses to our circumstances may change for the better. Therefore, cognitive theory also implies that the art of being a positive person with good self-esteem and confidence is based on our having positive cognitive perceptions of ourselves and of how others view us. *But, how do we 'find' these?*

Schema theory suggests that one's belief systems and potential outcomes from those beliefs are deeply rooted and enmeshed within one's personality, upbringing, interaction with family and peers and personal decisions. It proposes that these are evident in what one experiences in one's valued outcomes (or the means we use to access the end result we want).

The term *schemata* (Piaget 1954) is used to illustrate how one might access the scheme of things and lay down the foundation for core belief systems within the brain. It suggests that such core belief systems are routes or tracks that become established over time and are not easily remedied or challenged. In fact it is usual for one to maintain the status quo in order for one's body and mind to feel 'right'. For example, an individual controlled by an abandonment schema might believe the following: 'I know ultimately my friends will reject me; so I will keep them at a safe distance and not allow them to get too close to me.' Although this thinking might be at a subconscious level it is acted out in daily relationships. The action from the abandonment schema will send a message to the friends of the individual concerned and they will perceive that they are not valued as friends and may eventually leave the friendship. Their responses confirm the thinking of the individual: 'Yep, you see, I knew you would leave me.' And so this keeps the belief going that they will always, ultimately, be abandoned by everyone.

Another example of schemata or beliefs that hold us prisoner to our circumstances is found in the story told by Plato. We call this Plato's 'Cave Mentality'. Plato tells the story of a group of people who dwell in a cave and have never seen the light outside of their cave. One of them, however, ventures forth and courageously explores beyond the cave. As he climbs up and up he discovers daylight and the vast world outside of the cave. Although he is not accustomed to the light and, at first, it hurts his eyes, he perseveres and is overjoyed with what he experiences. Full of enthusiasm he travels back down to the others to share his joy with them. He tells them of the glorious light and openness beyond the cave. But they respond with fear and anger. They tell him of his foolishness and of all the comforts they have in the cave and refuse to hear him. So, we each are faced with a choice. Will we move towards the light we don't know or stay hidden in the shadows of where we think we know life and safety?

Taking the road less travelled (or moving towards understanding of self)

Working towards understanding one's belief systems and subsequent actions can be likened to opening a door that leads one on a positive journey towards self-acceptance. It may, therefore, help in shaping an inclusive societal pathway allowing for wider understanding and belonging. What starts with one individual such as you or me could ultimately assist society to recognize a more appropriate picture of normal and set a course for a more whole and inclusive future. Thus, it will not only give the opportunity to individuals to take back the control over their own lives, as opposed to being controlled by the past and the schemas occupying cognitive and emotive development, but will also add to the weight of communal understanding that aims to build a more inclusive society from the roots upward.

So, being able to visualize the cognitive and schematic processes involved with the development of understanding normal and rewrite them into one's individual and societal subconscious will open doors for a healthier life concept. When one considers that most neurologically typically developing individuals (usual term used for normal people) function best in the social arena with the developing knowledge that self is a reflection of societal norms, customs, traditions and accepted practices, then it is no wonder that normal has so many connotations and multi-sided aspects to it. The difficulty for some of us, however, is that normal is not inclusive of difference and in its most rigid form perpetuates modes of behaviour that prevent the healthy development of positive self-esteem and ability in a varied and wide population of individuals.

The arguments and ideas outlined in this chapter have tried to show how psychology and social constructs have impacted upon developing concepts of normal. They have also commented on the role the media and big business have in the high stakes of maintaining those concepts. It takes courage to stand up and take stock of one's life and to question one's beliefs. In the light of what you have read so far, I can only encourage you to read on and to explore with me just what truly constitutes 'normality'.

CHAPTER 2

Developing Concepts of the Autistic and Typical Spectrums

Just as in the previous chapter we saw how societal norms have been impacted upon and how they have changed over time, so we can see how this has also impacted upon our current understanding of autism and of the expectations placed upon us all, autistic or typical. This chapter will outline the current concepts of autism and show how they also have changed and how the idea of attention, as a limited but renewable resource, is implicated in both typical and autistic learning styles.

The spectrum of autism

Autism, which includes a variety of developmental labels, including Asperger's disorder, is proving to be quite an enigma for so many families. As an individual with autism, I find it quite difficult to read people's intentions and the assumptions they seem to make. I may miss the messages given by body language and find facial expressions hard to interpret. Therefore, I rely more heavily upon verbal scripts and less upon the ability to read others' body language. This is usual, typical and normal for me. But is this deviation from the norm or part of neural diversity? I certainly believe individuals may qualify for the label 'deviant', but they don't have to be autistic to do so. In fact, if one is to believe the television news, it would seem most deviant individuals are on the typical spectrum (TS).

According to current British statistics, as many as 1 in 58 children will be somewhere on the autistic spectrum (Baron-Cohen, Scott and

Stott 2007). One could argue that autism presents a picture of individuals who have huge difficulties in the everyday activities that others take for granted, therefore it must be a disorder. I would like to offer a different viewpoint and explanation of our difficulties. First, however, I will give you the current traditional description of the autism spectrum, which, for the purposes of this book, includes Asperger's disorder, classic (Kanner-type) autism, pervasive developmental disorder and autistic characteristics and/or atypical autism.

We will start with Asperger's disorder, one of the terms traditionally used for high-functioning autism. According to the *Diagnostic and Statistical Manual of Mental Disorders* (American Psychiatric Association 1994) for a diagnosis of Asperger's disorder to be made, the following must be present:

- a qualitative impairment in social interaction as manifested by at least two of the following: marked impairment in the use of multiple non-verbal behaviours (e.g. eye contact, gestures); failure to develop age-appropriate peer relationships; lack of spontaneous seeking to share interests or achievements with others; and lack of social or emotional reciprocity
- restricted repetitive and stereotyped patterns of behaviours, interests and activities as manifested by at least one of the following: preoccupation with at least one stereotyped and restricted pattern of interest (e.g. interest is obsessional and excludes all else) to an abnormal degree; inflexible adherence to non-functional routines or rituals; stereotyped and repetitive motor mannerisms; and preoccupation with parts of objects.

There must additionally be clinically significant impairment in social, occupational or other functioning; and no clinically significant delay in language, cognitive development, adaptive behaviour, or curiosity about the environment. Although Asperger's disorder is likely to be diagnosed in individuals who have traditionally been labelled as having 'high-functioning autism', they do not appear to have language impairments (Howlin 2003).

I want to add that, even though the above is taken directly from the traditional literature, there is a move afoot to focus more on AS strengths rather than deficits. Some researchers are claiming that AS is a cognitive style that appears to develop along a particular trajectory, meaning that one should focus upon its enabling abilities and not its deficiencies (Björne 2007; Happé and Frith 2006; Lawson 2001).

In some of the early literature, 'Kanner-type' autism is regarded as an unchangeable condition (Kanner 1943). However, many researchers today (e.g. Ghaziuddin 2005; Gillberg and Wing 1999; Prior 2003; Wing 1988) agree that autism is a continuum of characteristics with several overlapping aspects of cognitive and physiological behaviour found in both Kanner-type autism and in Asperger-type autism. Therefore, autism is currently viewed as having evolved from a 'black and white' concept to the idea of an autistic continuum (Wing 1992).

Should we, therefore, suggest that if you are closer to one end of that continuum, rather than the other, you are closer to normal? This really worries me! Are you normal if you talk and not normal if you don't? The first time I observed a group of deaf youth signing to each other it looked quite odd to me. I even felt uncomfortable because I couldn't relate to them. However, they were very much at home with one another and signing was very normal for them!

Some researchers (e.g. Attwood 1998; Rickarby, Carruthers and Mitchell 1991) have also suggested that children with AS move through the continuum. That is, for example, a child of four with a diagnosis of classic autism may appear closer to that of a child with Asperger's disorder at 14 years of age. However, even though AS and the idea of an autism continuum are relatively new concepts in the literature, narrative stories of individual lives demonstrate that the continuum has always existed (Gerland 1997; Grandin 1996; Lawson 2000; Williams 1994).

Even Kanner (1971) noted that children from his original study, on a follow-up study nearly 30 years later, were markedly different in that they had developed many abilities not seen initially. So, evidence for a 'continuum' in AS has existed since this condition was first noted as 'autism'. Therefore, today, the literature appears to suggest that AS is no longer a rare disorder with clearly defined narrow boundaries

(Attwood 2006; Manjiviona and Prior 1995; Waterhouse 2000; Wing 1988), but is a multi-faceted and complicated array of particular characteristics that change over time.

When one considers the literature on developmental hurdles and milestones that TS individuals go through during their lifetime, one could argue that the above could be true for so many other families, even those without an autistic diagnosis! This begs the questions 'What is normal?' and 'Who designed the goalposts?' For a fuller explanation of this comment please see Chapter 7 by Dinah Murray.

AS and gender

Baron-Cohen (2003, 2005) has argued that individuals have a male brain, female brain, or a balance of the two. It is suggested that individuals with AS, irrespective of their gender, will have more of what Baron-Cohen identifies as 'systemizing' characteristics and less of 'empathizing' characteristics. These characteristics are found in the male-oriented brain and Baron-Cohen suggests that individuals with AS have the extreme form of the male brain. If we are to argue concepts of normality are associated with brain difference (we know male and female brains are different) then as the autism campaigner Michelle Dawson has pointed out (in a video produced by the Pervasive Developmental Disorders Specialized Clinic, Hôpital Rivière-des-Prairies, University of Montreal) 'either the male brain or the female brain is deviant, depending on which one is your standard'.

To date, the literature exploring AS-related gender issues, such as AS being a predominantly male condition or, specifically, whether girls with autism present differently to boys, is scant (Attwood 1998, 2006). Gender impacts upon typical expression in any given population, therefore it is possible that it impacts upon expression in AS too. For example, girls are prone to being less aggressive in social play than boys, and these traits are seen in AS too (Attwood 1992). Boys may come to the attention of a parent, teacher or doctor because of their 'inappropriate' behaviour. Girls, who may choose solitude or books above social relationships, might be seen as 'bright, intelligent or loners' (Attwood 1992). According to Attwood (1998) when one compares the social worlds of girls with AS to those of boys with AS, the natural disposition towards social ability in girls is carried over, albeit at a reduced level, into the world of AS.

> Girls tend to be relatively more able in social play and have a more even profile of social skills. ...girls with Asperger's disorder seem more able to follow social actions by delayed imitation; however, their actions are not so well timed and spontaneous. (p.151)

It would seem that AS females are generally more drawn to the world of words and related interests (Marano 2005). However, Grandin (1995), a well-known autistic woman whose profession and practical know-how has revolutionized animal welfare with regard to husbandry and slaughter, finds writing and words quite difficult; nonetheless she has written three books that give insight into her world as an autistic individual. So, maybe autistic individuals of either gender vary in this regard too? Quite often I hear someone suggest that all autistic individuals are great at map reading and with interests concerning numbers. In the typical population these are often considered male pursuits. I am female, autistic and hopeless with numbers and with maps! We are all so different. In fact I once heard a well-known professional say 'autistics are more different than they are alike'.

Attwood (1998) suggests that girls with a diagnosis of AS in their primary years may progress along the autism continuum so well that by the time they are teenagers, the current diagnostic criteria for AS will fail to address the social and communicative difficulties they experience. That is, their level of perceived 'ability' will mask their true difficulties. I am, however, left wondering if this might not also be the case for many other individuals, even if they are typical. That is, how many TS individuals have difficulties they cover up or don't share with others?

Current research by Carter *et al.* (2007) shows female toddlers with autism being less socially competent than the boys. They are also better at non-verbal problem-solving than the boys:

> The findings revealed a statistically significant interaction between child sex and cognitive domain (verbal versus nonverbal) and child sex and the 5 Mullen Scales of Early Learning (Visual Reception, Fine

> Motor, Expressive Language, Receptive Language, and Gross Motor), indicating that girls and boys with ASD show different cognitive and developmental profiles. Consistent with the expectation that boys would show more advanced development, boys evidenced stronger verbal and motor skills, particularly once differences in visual reception were covaried. Controlling for language level, girls evidenced significantly stronger skills in visual reception, or the nonverbal problem solving domain. In addition, boys were described as having more advanced social functioning than girls. (p.94)

As Petra Björne (2007) has pointed out:

> This all runs contrary to Baron-Cohen's idea of the male brain. Or, if you wish, the girls are more male than the boys. Given the fact that there are so very few studies addressing the cognitive profiles of autism from a gender perspective, it is important that the popular accounts are modified somewhat by more rigorous studies. (Personal communication)

It seems that, whatever one's gender, if we are somewhere on the spectrum of autism our thinking and problem-solving abilities differ from those of the typical world. However, just because one is different or arrives at an understanding by taking a different route, this doesn't mean there isn't value in our processing or problem-solving attributes. It makes no sense to say that, just because we didn't do something typically, we did it wrong! (See Mottron *et al.* 2004 and 2007.)

Deviation or neural diversity?

Could it not be that the desire in any given population might be to 'fit in' and 'belong' to such an extent that one learns to wear the social smile and mask the real difficulties and fears that one has? Perhaps the only difference is that in autism one doesn't attempt to 'hide' but is truer to one's real identity. If being normal means hiding one's real self, what is the ultimate point? Surely it takes courage and strength of character to be 'real' in a world that only welcomes pretence, pressure and propensity to please!

Please accept me

I'm not the same on the outside as I am on the inside. I smile, I laugh, but I don't know joy. Where is my joy? I try to watch from a safe distance, but nothing seems safe. I used to feel a sense of freedom. I could flick my fingers in front of my face to make the scenery change – like many still pictures become a film when flicked through quickly. This action creates a sense of movement whilst keeping still. When it was only me no one else mattered, it was as if they did not exist. Everything was once so free. Once grass was green and hills were inviting. Now they are covered with mist and veiled in smog. The greyness forbids me. What was once clear is now murky and unsure.

Inside is cold, tight and sad. I cry; I ache. Most days I long for eyes to see me, but I stay hidden. I have to hide where none can see. For, if they see me they will despise me. 'Help' I say inside my prison. I scream, but upon my face I smile. If you were to look more closely at my eyes you might see the pain. Maybe it's just too uncomfortable for you. You see, if you notice my pain, you might feel obliged to do something about it. This would take effort and mean you might become unpopular yourself... I wouldn't want to disturb your equilibrium.

I've been brave; I've tried. But from openness comes pain. There are those who want to close my door; who trample my little girl. So light and gay is she, but oh so sensitive. Too many times others have driven her in. 'Come out, little girl' I coax, but she just sits and mopes. No longer can I coax her out. 'Are you sleeping, little girl?' Lord, send someone to love her to life once more. (Lawson 2007, p.20)

The spectrum of typical development

Just as there is a spectrum of autism, I believe there is a spectrum of typical development. TS development is thought of as the developing ability to do certain things at certain times, in a particular progression and time period. In layman's terms we call these 'milestones': for example, learning to join another individual's attention and share information (interests). Have you ever taken a small child for a walk? If so, you might hold their hand and talk to them as you walk. You might point things out to the child and the child might share the moment with you. When walking along a country lane with my children when they were small I often commented on things we passed. 'Look at the tractor,' I might say; 'Look at the train'; 'Look at the pony.' Children typically follow the direction of an adult's gaze or finger that acts as a means to point something out to them.

Language development in typical children usually involves the child developing single words for things that interest them and stringing them into sentences to use them appropriately. They also develop shared interests and learn how to take turns at play with other children. Listening to others, understanding other points of view and developing a sense of self and of other are all aspects of typical human development that require an interaction between cognitive, emotional and social understanding.

To access these domains for learning in the typical style, the human brain develops the capacity for dividing attention. Divided attention means the ability to attend to several things simultaneously: for example, to look, listen, touch and taste all at once. This capacity allows typical individuals to access information via their senses, process it cognitively and then act upon it in whatever capacity they deem fit for the purpose. This might mean muscle activity, such as the physical action of movement, or it might mean cognitive activity, such as thought. In typical individuals, the dual process of feeling and thinking is taken for granted and even expected. Toddlers as young as 18 months can separate talking from walking, from listening, and so on.

There are several outcomes from this ability to divide attention, and becoming a social being is a natural outcome of typical development. A social being is one who employs social objectives that allow them to conform to social norms, behave with appropriate morality and adhere to the social conscience of the society they are part of. For many typical individuals, however, the term 'social' extends beyond these borders into 'being social is seen as a priority'. Therefore, interaction with others, especially as part of a group, is thought of as desirable. Unfortunately, though, desirable develops in one's mind to become 'the norm'. When this is taken even further it becomes abnormal when one does not want to join a group and prefers to be on one's own. This mistaken concept of 'social humanity' has become embedded in most of our current institutions; for example, family. Family should always be a 'safe place' where one can be oneself, even if that means being happy to be alone.

Another aspect of social and emotional development is in knowing what is expected in particular situations. For example, when is it okay for one person to share private information with another person? Even knowing what is private and what is public depends upon this growing awareness of self and of other.

Social compliance and social deception depend upon the ability to divide one's attention so one can be alert to a number of different variables. For example, children as young as three years old, when told not to look behind themselves to see what a particular toy might be, were found to have looked when they believed that no one could see that they had (Lewis *et al.* 1989). This ability to 'notice' and work out what they could 'get away with', and then allow the researcher to believe they had not looked (even when they had), requires the individual to attend to a number of different stimuli – both seen and not seen, presumed and worked out from states such as curiosity, boredom, expectation and desire to play with the toy as well as the desire to please the adult. A state of polytropism (a processing resource including divided attention governed by a diverse and diffuse interest system) (Murray 1992) is assumed for this to occur in typical children.

One of the usual developments seen as a result of typical development and growth in children is the concept of 'play'. Children who play well appear to be better equipped for adult life. Many researchers have stressed the importance of play, of narrative and of literacy, as children interact with one another or with their own 'play' (e.g. Christie and Enz 1993; Einarsdottir 2000; Mahoney and Powell 1988; Neuman and Roskos 1992; Piers and Landau 1980; Russ 1993; Stone and Christie 1996).

> One of the fundamental functions of play is the way it unconsciously provides a narrative that consciously transforms thoughts and action. This is because play contains within it the same elements of timing, role and emotion that form any narrative structure. (Seach 2007, p.76)

Cognitively, however, the ability to divide one's attention is critical to typical development. Having a diffuse/diverse interest system and being able to access multiple interests (one's own and others) relies upon the developing ability to divide one's attention and build connections between mind and emotion – between his and hers; between up, over, under, through; yours, mine, ours, theirs; feelings, thoughts and movement, to name but a few. Even forward thinking requires the ability to divide one's attention because it presupposes a state of knowing the difference between 'now' and 'then'.

Key developmental differences between AS and TS

It is reasonable to state with regard to social and emotional development that, because AS individuals are not typically developing, they and the typical world are confused by one another. For typical development to occur successfully, there needs to be a connection between the ability to divide one's attention and the ability to access a multiple-diffuse interest system. This then has impact upon one's learning style. For example, typical individuals have a learning style that enables them to connect to the visual, auditory, kinaesthetic, social and emotional world within themselves and without. It enables them to note and model other people's interests so that they share and communicate in similar ways to those around them. This type of learning requires attention, interest and interplay between senses and cognition.

Individuals receive information through their senses allowing them to processes that information (smell, hear, feel, taste, judge distance, and so on) and respond to it. In typical individuals this sensory processing occurs simultaneously with cognitive translation. However, in AS it is more usual for individuals to use single attention with emphasis upon a non-diffuse interest system (monotropism), which results in one's 'senses' working independently rather than together. In typical development, integrated sensory function is primary to typical growth and development (Björne 2007; Bogdashina 2003).

The paper by Rutherford *et al.* (2007) on divided attention in AS showed that AS individuals were more accurate (than controls) at a divided attention task, using a useful field of view (UFOV) task to show visual processing and attention shifting between global and local stimuli. Although this result was unexpected and seemed to contradict previous research, the authors did comment that simply locating and spotting the visual stimuli (a test for divided attention) was not the same as noting them for meaning. It could be that a factor not accounted for in their testing was that of the connection the interest system plays in the role of attention. For example, in autism as well as in typicality, one is more likely to note or recognize an element if one's interest is stimulated, and one is more likely to build connections between elements if one is interested in that connection.

Therefore, if the above is true (partly because of the role of interest and its connection to attention), and if as 'AS individuals' our interest is not 'sparked', there might be a lack of social and spontaneous interaction. This would explain why, among other things, we often appear to have a preference for similarity rather than variety and our literal interpretation of human behaviour places some limitation on our fantasy or theatrical imaginations.

AS individuals' behaviour is often written about as one might write about 'loners' who have problems when placed in group activities. Reading the intentions of others and knowing what this might mean for them and for us is difficult for us. This means we have lots of difficulties working out the changing roles of individuals we relate to and, as a coping strategy, will often resist change. In so many ways this behaviour is different to behaviour found in typical individuals. Therefore, typical individuals and autistic individuals will find each other's behaviour difficult to understand.

However, when interest is added to the equation, play and social activity can develop meaning for AS individuals, and allow for mutual social interaction. For example, Stagnitti (personal communication, 2007), with reference to Merchant (2006), found that when three principles of 'play' were consistently and steadily taught to autistic children during a pilot intervention programme and subsequent follow-up programmes, the children learned to play, and to play like a typical child might. The three principles used included the child's interest (to enable shared attention), motivation (through interest), and the application of these to problem solving.

Individuals who develop typically do so as their experience is informed by certain cognitive processes. They observe and filter information from their senses and make use of it according to need or desire.

As previously stated, they may become good at attending to differing stimuli that present to them and develop the ability to divide their attention and interests between a number of different tasks. This polytropic ability enables typical individuals to share their world with those around them and to join the attention of others (to have multiple-diffuse interests) if they choose to. In so doing, the social currency of shared language (verbal and body) and experiences enables typical individuals to enter the world of social understanding. Usually they do this more readily than AS individuals because their particular learning styles foster the art of what it means to be a sociable being inclusive of group activity and often outside of one's own interest. In practical terms, this allows many typical individuals to understand 'small-talk', political diplomacy and the many reasons one tells oneself that it's okay to be dishonest when it's for a good cause! Whereas, AS individuals always have to tell the truth. Unfortunately, our honesty can be interpreted as deviant.

AS individuals also develop as their experiences are informed by certain cognitive and sensory processes. However, unlike typical individuals, AS individuals use monotropic attention (single attention allowing highly focused interests to take precedence). Thus, they tend to be single-minded and do not divide their attention very easily. According to Murray *et al.* (2005), this accounts for much of the clinical picture we see in AS (e.g. resistance to change, obsessive behaviours, non-social priorities, egocentricity, and so on).

The above profile in AS individuals is the result of our brain development. Research shows that brain development in AS individuals is different to that of typical individuals (e.g. Baron-Cohen 2003). It is for this reason that the social world might not make much sense to AS individuals and social skill acquisition might be difficult. However, when our individual learning styles are valued and accommodated, it will simply mean that our interests will be used as a medium to access learning. This could mean a whole different ball game and one that we can share with each other, whether typical or autistic.

This chapter has briefly outlined AS and TS development and shown these concepts have changed over time. Keeping an open mind on these issues and appreciating just what a difference valuing and accommodating different learning styles might mean for individuals could mean the difference between a positive or a negative future.

CHAPTER 3

The Individual, Family and Society

More on How Ideas of Normality Have Changed

Recently my daughter gave birth to a beautiful baby girl. One of the first things the parents did was to check their new little person over and enquire of the midwives that her 'bits were all there' and that 'she was all right'. Within our concepts of normal we have a particular view of 'physical' normality. This means having the right amount of digits at the end of one's limbs; two eyes, a nose and mouth; a body in proportion to one's head; being a particular length; having the appropriate gender assignment; and having all the right reflexes.

Maybe the idea that one's body has to be a certain way in order to be normal and to have a normal life has been perpetuated over time due to the increased likelihood of employment and relationship opportunity being afforded in one's future. Disability, even having a stammer or poor eyesight, was seen throughout history as a blemish upon society. This meant that children born or developing any such blemish were often not expected to thrive, and some families covered their 'shame' by keeping such children hidden. In Victorian times it was normal for one in five children to die, and many children, especially if disabled in any way, were not expected to live past their fifth birthday.

Once upon a time, being left-handed was considered abnormal, and left-handed individuals were thought of as not trustworthy and not very bright! Desks at universities did not accommodate left-handedness, scissors were only made for right-handed people and, unless you were famous, you could not purchase a guitar designed to be played left-handed! Today in Western culture we would not dream of penalizing someone because they were left-handed. Rather, we would see the individual and their 'right' to an education where being left-handed was irrelevant.

On a recent Channel 4 documentary (NAS 2007) someone stated that it might not be appropriate to think of autism as a 'difference' or a 'different culture' (rather than a disability), because individuals with complex needs might not get the support they need. My question is 'Why?' If typical individuals require optical support (for example) to enable them to see better, do we say 'Because you are not disabled, just a bit short-sighted, you don't have the right to spectacles'? No, we don't say that. We say 'You need glasses. It's important that you should see better. You have a right to such support.' The autism researcher Michelle Dawson in an interview has said that: 'we each have the right to exist as ourselves'. Being autistic is normal for me. I do need support, yes, but who doesn't? I don't think any of us was created to live totally independently. Rather, we are each created for community and interdependence. It's okay to need others in one's life!

If one happens to be differently abled, or have a physical body that places more limitations upon it than most others experience (e.g. cerebral palsy) and one needs a wheelchair for mobility, it could be argued that this is normal for that individual. My elderly mother needs a walking frame to assist her in moving from place to place. The frame lends her the support she needs now that her legs are less strong and her balance less steady. Does this make my mother 'not normal'? No, a walking frame is normal for Mum.

We need to redefine normal by placing it into context, place and time. It is normal for my mum to have a cup of tea in the morning, with milk and no sugar. It isn't normal for me though; I always have a cup of coffee in the morning, not tea. If we added up all the individuals who drank white tea (black tea with milk) and compared them to coffee drinkers it would become obvious that tea drinking isn't normal in America, even if it is in the UK. We might even go a step further and state that tea drinkers are abnormal, or one needs to be abnormal to drink tea in the morning and not coffee!

It was once odd to see someone standing on a platform at a railway station waiting for a train and talking to themselves. In today's world this is totally acceptable, because we assume that such an individual is not mad, but is talking on a mobile phone. Normality and appearance of normality in this regard have certainly changed during the past decade. Using mobile phones (to text others, take photographs, set up an itinerary and organize one's day, do calculations and help with budgeting, record names, numbers, addresses and e-mail addresses) is part of modern technology. One can even use a mobile phone to telephone another person and chat to them!

'If it's right, it's my right, it's all right.' No, that isn't right. I say this because we all have 'rights', but they vary across populations, generations and expectations. Therefore, maybe the right 'right' is to be considerate of the rights of others and not only the 'right' of self. In a society where one's instant gratification has become one's right, it is fashionable to put 'self' first. What is fashionable becomes 'the norm' and, unfortunately, this type of norm eats away at the very fabric of society.

Difference (my normality)

Difference, in the shape of physical or mental form, culture, religion, intellect, education, belief systems and gender disposition, does not have to be seen as being in opposition to the usual and normal wellbeing of society as a whole. Incorporating individual 'difference' into societal life, however, might mean necessitation of my difference becoming visible, and I will need to show the world what I require to enable me to live life normally for me. A new friend of mine, 'Kell', from Rockhampton in Queensland, said to me this morning when she was giving me a lift to the airport:

> Wendy, our families should be places where we know we are able to be ourselves. The family is like a big pond where the supportive edges are clear, but where, as we bring others into that pond, there is a ripple-on effect that moves out to impact positively upon others.

This is one of the ways we foster inclusion. Good on ya, Kell!

An autistic friend of mine was asked if she were offered a pill to cure her autism, would she take it. She replied that she enjoyed her life with autism at home because it meant she could 'play with her beloved toys and flappies' and she wouldn't want to give that up. However, she added, if she could take a pill that took away her fear of life outside of home, she would take it.

How many of us, autistic or not, are fearful of public opinion, of getting it wrong, of being misjudged, of not being accepted, of not fitting in, and so on? Maybe we need less medical intervention and more societal acceptance. Maybe we need to work on building up our confidence, our self-esteem and our acceptance of self. It is a fact that, if we are confident and appear self-assured, others respect and admire us. At times it seems we might need to 'fake it to make it'.

Having said this, of course, many of us have a disability that means we need support to do the regular things that others take for granted. This isn't being difficult and not trying to manage on one's own, it's because our particular disability leaves us with a handicap that requires particular intervention and support. In certain events, such as horse racing, 'handicaps' are awarded and jockeys carry more or less weight so that all horses and jockeys have an even advantage. No one would dispute this, it's normal practice. Yet accommodating one's 'handicap' in everyday life has become an issue that individuals have felt the need to politicize. In order to access education, shops, public transport and, for some, one's own home, it seems it is normal that one has to fight for recognition and equality. For some of us, fighting the status quo requires just too much energy and, once we have gotten through our daily routines, we don't have any energy left over!

So this is me

Fair skinned and freckled, podgy, pedantic and particular, that's me.
Dark hair, not so tall, I need glasses to help me see.
I rescue beetles, ants and spiders,
I love water, shades and 'Sliders'.
Science fiction, books about nature, birds, butterflies and bush.
Pussy cats, dogs, sunshine and rainbows,
These are the things that turn me to mush.

I don't like mathematics; numbers make me hurt.
Can't trust me with money or leave me with the purse.

Saddened by indifference, intolerance and pain,
Happy to be autistic, glad to be on this train.

So what does it mean to be a normal individual? Even societal concepts of 'normal individual' will change over time. Time changes concepts almost naturally, as individual knowledge and experiences add weight to what is known and understood. At one time, scientists believed that women were of 'lesser' intelligence and more prone to hysteria than men were. A woman's womb was believed to be the seat of her *hysterical* disposition (from the Greek word *hustera* meaning 'womb'). We no longer believe that women are of lesser intelligence than men; we now understand that intelligence is not defined by one's gender. However, some societies still believe that male children are of more value than female children. The only way that this will change is by women showing themselves to be valuable and capable, not as someone's asset or property but as individuals in their own right. In some societies this will take immense courage and commitment.

Whenever one looks at nature and the natural world around us it soon becomes obvious that male and female roles are different. But how clear is this, and is it different for different species or does it stay the same each time for every one? Are males always stronger, bigger, more physical and more focused? If you are a black widow spider, the answer is no! In the black widow species of spider the male is smaller, less dangerous and not so well equipped to live as long as his female counterpart. In fact, after mating with her (if she doesn't eat him first) he has to be very quick not to become her next meal. In order to live, he must convince her of his usefulness and almost lull her into a belief that she will not want to eat him. Who said women had the monopoly on manipulative behaviours!

Yes, it is usual for women to be less physically strong than men, generally. We know that typically a woman's body is designed with curves and less rigidity, and is adapted for childbirth. Males, in the human population, might need to be physically strong to attract and then protect their mates and offspring. They don't need the body design of a female, so each is designed to complement the other. But, is this where it ends? No, of course it isn't.

It is clear that individuals do not come in standard sizes or even with standard equipment, personalities or repertories of language, phrases or communication styles. Individuals even have their own unique learning styles, and no one person is exactly the same as another. Yet, even though this seems like common sense, we still find it difficult to accept someone who is not like ourselves. Maybe they don't agree with our views on sport, politics, fashion or philosophy. Maybe they are a different colour, or from a different culture, religion or belief system. But, rather than see that this is who they are and accept these things as being part of their normal experience, we accommodate our fears and discomforts by discrediting the other person. It's unfortunately not uncommon to hear comments like 'Oh well, he's from the poor side of town, so he isn't very bright'; 'Oh, he's Scottish so he's very tight and I wouldn't trust him'; 'Oh, women drivers...they always hog the road'; and so on.

If we want to see this kind of thinking and behaviour change then we need to be involved as part of the solution. Being autistic is different, but it doesn't mean that it's bad. I recognize that I am disabled in a world that does not recognize, respect, value and accommodate difference. However, for my learning style to be appreciated and for me to be free to access the tools I need to make my daily life liveable and not too stressful, I need to become visible. I also need to accept others and respect who they are.

Many individuals are afraid of 'autism' because they don't understand our behaviour. Perhaps this is one of the reasons they want to make autism go away? I think it would be better to begin by accepting who I am, and then develop a way for us both to communicate so we can build a future together where we can both feel comfortable. After all, we accept that some people love cars and engines whilst others prefer books. So why is it so hard to accept that I like to flap my hands, rock a little or enjoy a special interest?

Whose family life?

As a young teenager I had a friend who came from quite a 'well to do' family. One afternoon I was invited to join them for afternoon tea, then stay to dinner and spend the night as my friend's guest. I was very much looking forward to being with my friend and getting to know her family a little. However, when I went to my friend's home it seemed so different to my own. I was unsure of so many things and found it quite difficult to 'feel at home'.

In my friend's home, upon entering the house one removed one's shoes. We didn't do this in my home. The house seemed quite 'grand' to me, with antique furniture, wonderful oil paintings on the walls of large rooms and hallways, a separate laundry, even two spare guest rooms that came with their own bathrooms! My home was a terraced house with three bedrooms. We rented the house from the council, and no one in my family, at that time, would have dreamed of ever owning their own home. Our washing machine was in the kitchen under the bench, and we all shared one bathroom. In our lounge room (we only had one, not like my friend who had a regular lounge and a formal lounge) the telly was always on. When the football results were being given out, God help any individual who spoke out loud! In my friend's home the television was contained within a special cabinet with doors that were kept closed when the television wasn't in use. Which of these family homes is normal? Well, of course, they both are.

Family life isn't only about home life, though, it's about the individuals who make up the family. The majority of children start out having two parents. Some get to stay with their two parents for many years. Others, however, for a variety of reasons, end up living with just one parent. Do children who live with two parents fare better than children who live with one? The literature isn't convincing on this issue. There are so many factors to consider.

Sometimes even though children live with two parents, one parent might feel that they do all the parenting. At other times, unfortunately, the home is the seat of domestic violence, and when the two parents are together family life is very stressful and difficult. In theory, the idea of having children together with another person and sharing the responsibility is noble. However, in practice it might not work out that way. Sometimes, when family life breaks down, the children can become pawns in a battle between adults. This is really unfair and unethical! However, all of the above are normal family states for countless families in Western society. It would be lovely to think that the ideal family and the normal family are one and the same, but this just isn't true for many households.

Some of my friends were not born in Australia but migrated from other countries. Although they are Australian residents and many have taken up Australian citizenship, they tend not to eat typical Australian tucker. Take my friend 'Jo' for example. Jo eats lots of curry, rice and flat bread. This is normal in Jo's family and he enjoys it. Jo's parents have never eaten pizza and say they are not likely to! So, you see what is normal for one family might not be normal for another. The good news is that Jo's family don't mind that I don't eat lots of curry, and understand that my family likes pizza; they also don't mind that Jo eats pizza with my family at times too.

It's good to accommodate each other's likes and dislikes, and learn to get along with one another. One of the reasons I love to watch *Star Trek* on TV is because the characters are often so different from one another, not just in culture and hobbies or interests, but also in physical appearance, gender roles, beliefs, social expectations and even greeting habits. The programme helped me to accept that what is normal for me might not be normal for someone else, and I learnt to be more tolerant of difference.

Institutional 'family' life

This morning I was in the university library researching through journal articles with a friend. I'm accustomed to having a coffee break between 10.30am and 11am. In Australia it's normal to call this 'morning tea' or 'smoko'. It used to be normal for students to gather and have a cigarette with a cup of coffee, but these days it's regarded as antisocial to smoke in public places, even forbidden in most, so fewer students are smoking in a group. Whereas it was once difficult to find a smoke-free room to sit in, now it's difficult to find somewhere to smoke! I am happy about the new rules with regards to smoking because I find smoke from cigarettes quite uncomfortable, but it's interesting that what was once considered normal is now abnormal.

Whilst standing at the Kiosk counter waiting for my cup of coffee, another customer gave their order. I was interested to note that they asked for 'a normal coffee please'. I had asked for a latte (normal coffee to me) but these days you can get coffees in a variety of guises. There's a 'flat white', a tall or short black, a cappuccino, a latte, an espresso, a mocha with cream, a single shot or a double shot (the list goes on); and you can have it 'take away' or drink in! You can also get cold or hot coffee and you can get it mixed with a variety of other things, like an Irish coffee that comes with a shot of whisky.

When I was growing up, it was normal to have Camp coffee, which came in a narrow-necked bottle, as a liquid. One simply boiled water and added milk and sugar to taste. With regard to normal, where coffee is concerned, things have certainly changed.

Institutions, such as university and college, have changed with time, but only very slowly. Within Western society once it was normal for only boys to receive an education; now it is normal for anyone who qualifies for tertiary education to go to university or college. It doesn't matter what gender you are or what your age is. Education is seen as a right for all. However, some of the institutional ways of doing things have continued on down through the ages. One still 'gowns up' to graduate from university, and the order of qualification and status hasn't changed at all. I feel very much at home with my university family – so much so that I visit the campus and sit on the large lawned area just to feel 'connected' to life and reminded that I belong there. I once heard it said that universities are sheltered workshops for Asperger's individuals. Now that's a nice thought!

Another aspect to my institutional 'family' life is the way computers (and technology in general) have changed how I communicate with my peers and with colleagues around the world. When I was first an undergraduate, I hand-wrote my essays and spent many, many hours writing and re-writing. Then, the university passed a law that stated all essays had to be typed. I lack the coordination to touch type with fingers on both hands, so I had to learn to type with one finger.

Typing just wasn't normal for me! I persevered, because gaining an education in my area of interest was a dream for me that I wanted to pursue. These days I type, still with one finger, and it's just not normal for me to write with a pen any more! Now, some might argue that it's sad to lose this skill and be so dependent upon a machine to type words... I would argue that I'm pleased that this is now generally accepted and seen as a normal medium for written expression and wonder if it's not just a bit nostalgic to miss pen and ink. Surely, communicating in any form is the thing to be valued, rather than seeing one medium as being superior to any other?

Another form of institutional life that I have known is being in a hospital for long periods of time. I was in a regular ward with regular children who were sick. It was normal for us to be in a hospital routine and only have visits from adult family members for an hour in the afternoon. During one of my hospital stays, when I was nearly ten years old, I didn't see my siblings for almost a year. During this time, my sisters and brother had gotten on with life without me. It had become normal for them to be without their sister. Unfortunately for me, however, when I finally went home, my family and I were strangers to each other. Much of the 'normality' I had known before that time in the hospital was no longer considered normal. For example, instead of listening to the radio, my family now watched a television. When I walked around reading a book I was seen as 'unusual'. My parents used to say, 'Put the book down, Wendy, and come and watch this.'

I still love books, but I find myself really drawn to watching television. If the TV is on I find it very difficult not to look at it. It has become normal for me to enjoy watching certain television programmes, and I spend less time reading and even less time listening to the radio!

Deinstitutionalization

I know in recent times many institutions have closed down and individuals now live as part of their general communities. This could be a good thing, as long as those individuals have ways to understand today's current world. Unfortunately, resources and appropriate mediums for communicating one's needs have not kept pace. Technology could be a huge part of the answer to solving this issue. For example, via digital images on a computer one can familiarize oneself with new information, and this can help prepare for change. Mapping of areas, learning about what to expect with regard to physical domains and even working out social expectations can be explored on a computer that has internet access or appropriate software.

Technology is available, inexpensive and fashionable! For many AS individuals, technology can guide and support our continued learning, particularly of the social world. In many ways, it suits us better than many traditional modes of learning. Computers often make reading and writing more accessible. Where once we might have been quite stumped by the speed of reading and conversing expected of us, now there is a medium that allows it all to be slowed down sufficiently for us to process it better.

Technology is also helping me to integrate my 'difference' into the wider general society that I am part of. I have a web page and e-mail addresses that allow me to connect with others around the world. In this way I can share my interests (insects, birds, etc.) as well as ideas, opinions, understandings, and so on. I get to share in other people's stories as well. This is a good way to furnish and foster community, as well as build mutual awareness.

Difference

Difference, diversity, variety and all,
Help protect from boredom to keep us walking tall.

Otherwise, with head bowed down,
We walk in circles about town,
With no enthusiasm,
No reason to explore.

If you were me and I were you and all of us were the same,
Who would turn the lights off?
Who would end the game?

We need each other in various forms,
We need the jagged edges.
Just as queen and king need pawns,
And gardens may need hedges.

In fact it is quite normal,
As you can plainly see,
For each to need the other,
In a world of you and me.

So, when we take the ideas outlined in these first three chapters and apply them to our own developing and changing lives, it becomes obvious that we are all very different. This poses problems for creating some standard sense of 'normal', but it is clear that normal for each of us is also different. I propose one can be different but normal at the same time. Difference and usual are both constructs that sit on a continuum of normality because they are both experiences one has in everyday normal life.

CHAPTER 4

Difference, Normality and the Art of Conversation

A typical day

You might ask what relevance writing about a typical day might have for one person when, once again, it might not be another's typical day. I am writing about typicality, normal and usual and aiming to apply the concepts in as many ways as I can. Therefore, there is relevance in looking at someone's 'typical day'. I also have come to believe that how we start our day might have some bearing upon how the day proceeds, and on how we interact and converse with others. You might be aware of the idea that if one encounters a smile from another person then one is more likely to feel good, and if one encounters hostility one is likely to carry that over into the rest of the day.

A typical day for me begins when I wake up about 5am. I tend to go to bed late and wake early. I'm not a great sleeper, so my night-time sleep will be dotted with wakings, wanderings (to the bathroom or kitchen and back to my bed) and a small amount of sleeping. I often wake up completely and work on my computer for a while or read some pages from a favoured book of the moment. This is my usual night-time routine. However, it would not be normal for my partner to have sleep that is so interrupted and not continuous. In fact, compared to my sleep needs of about four hours, she needs eight hours. If her sleep was broken in the way mine is, she would be unable to function 'normally' the next day.

It seems two kinds of brain are normal with regard to sleeping. Some have the type of brain that allows for eight hours' sleep a night (or at another sleeping time that is usual for you) whilst others seem to need much less sleep and don't appear to suffer from sleep deprivation if they only have, say, four hours' sleep. But, if you have the type of brain that functions best with more sleep, rather than with less, you will notice the lack of sleep in your everyday life. The kind of brain needing eight hours' sleep is the kind of brain typically found in rodents. The kind of brain needing four hours' sleep tends to wake easily and is bright as a button straightaway, and is the kind of brain we find in dolphins. Either type of brain is normal for the individual concerned, but not normal in the other person. This might explain why some people seem so 'ratty' with one another!

It might also create difficulties for some lifestyles and for some individuals. My partner needs an alarm clock to wake her up (even then she might sleep through the noise of the alarm) but I usually wake up before any alarm goes off. I'm up and out of bed as soon as I wake up. My partner needs more time to get used to the idea that it's morning! If I attempt to chat to my partner in the morning before she has had her coffee, she might not really be up to following or joining my conversation. This discrepancy between whether one is a 'morning' person or not will impact upon one's ability to 'connect' to conversation and might mean conversations are typically missed, not listened to for meaning or are held 'loosely' by certain other individuals. If we appreciate these differences between us it should help us adjust to the different types of normal everyday conversations that we might find ourselves involved in (or not involved in as the case may be).

After waking I have quite a particular structure that I aim to follow for my day. The first thing I do is make myself a mug of instant coffee. It's strange to call it 'instant' coffee because I need to boil the water, pour it over the coffee powder, add milk and sugar, and then it's ready to drink. So, it's not really instant! My partner, however, dislikes coffee made this way. She doesn't think of this as 'real' coffee. Instead, she likes to freshly grind the coffee beans, place the ground coffee into her coffee-making machine (which has heated the water ready to filter through the ground coffee beans) and then press a control on her coffee machine that gives her an espresso coffee. Although both of these are different ways to enjoy coffee in the morning, one is normal to one individual but not normal to the other and vice versa!

So the day goes on. It's normal for me to eat breakfast before eight o'clock but not normal for some individuals who might not eat breakfast at all. It's normal for me to stay in my night clothes until I have a reason to get dressed. For others, though, getting dressed is the essential next step after getting up. So, if we each have different routines that are normal to each of us, how can we gauge what a normal conversation should consist of, especially when each individual has their own agenda, own sets of interests and own ways of thinking of things?

The essence of a normal conversation

With reference to the previous section one might conclude there is no such thing as a 'normal' conversation. In fact, I reckon talking out loud to myself helps me to gauge a conversation as opposed to jumping right on in there! But traditionally most conversations include someone else. While it can sometimes be helpful, and enable us to clarify our thoughts, to speak out loud to ourselves, it can be viewed as strange if we do it too often.

It seems people engage in conversation for a number of reasons. For example, lots of people feel good when they have been acknowledged by another. We say 'good day' to folks and smile at each other. It's one way we can share in our humble humanity. Another way we use speech is to share our thoughts, hopes, dreams, fears and ideas with someone else, in order to be heard by them and get feedback from them. Sayings such as 'a burden shared is a burden halved' have arisen from the activity of sharing one another's worlds. But, how did we learn to use speech this way? Is this the only reason we use speech?

Speech can be thought of, by those who are talkers, as the usual currency for exchange of interests and the communicating of one's needs and desires. In this instance an interest includes information, goals, thoughts, purposes, propositions, and so on. When I use speech I may draw attention away from what someone else was engaged in and onto what I want. It seems that from quite a young age typical individuals 'note and then model' other people's interests (Murray, personal communication, 2003). This is very useful because we can then make intelligent guesses about what we consider appropriate conversation. How does one know if it's the right time to talk about the weather, or if one should offer commiserations, congratulations, ruminations or just plain any old 'saytions'? We usually know because we have observed over many years the things others have done; we have been told what one should do and we learn to listen to our intuition too. If we realize that we have got it wrong, we may be quick to apologize, which gives us a second chance to get it right.

But if you are not typically developing then the outline above might not apply to you. Instead, if you are autistic, for example, you might not note and model other people's interests. Failure to note what appears to be happening for others will have all sorts of knock-on consequences. For example, someone might speak but we might not realize they are speaking to us! Even if we do notice they are speaking, we might not notice the content or tone of the speech. Therefore, it might mean our replies (if we reply) might not be guided by knowledge of the other person's conversation or expectation they may have of us. So, we could be perceived as being rude, insensitive, lazy, and so on. Of course, the latter might be the case for some individuals but, more often than not, we are simply unaware.

If awareness can be built between us, however, then the story might be quite different. I truly want to connect with my friends and share in things that affect their lives, because I care for them. But I'm not too good at engaging in things I'm not interested in – it somehow seems like being dishonest. But if my friends can find a way to capture my attention, then I can share the journey with them.

For example, one of my friends was raving on about members of her family. I wasn't interested because I just couldn't relate to what she was saying. Then this friend noticed my lack of interest and asked me if I was bored by her conversation. I told her I wasn't able to connect with what she was saying because it made no sense to me; there just wasn't anything about the conversation that captured my attention, so I couldn't relate to it! Upon hearing this, my friend began to find ways to relate the conversation to me by including examples of things that interested me. Because I was interested and, therefore, attentive, the conversation began to make sense to me. It also meant that

I was better at 'cottoning on' to what my friend was saying and could legitimately share in conversation with her without feeling as though I was lying!

You see, it's easier for me to relate once my attention and interest are 'sparked'. In fact, although it is normal and usual for individuals to converse about things that hold mutual interest, finding a way to do that in autism might not be the typical way. I say this because for those of us with AS, it's normal and usual for us only to talk about things that are of interest to us and to feel uncomfortable if we are asked to show interest in things that don't interest us. Therefore, it makes sense, when sharing in conversation with an AS individual, to encourage conversation by joining their interest first.

Recently I had an e-mail from someone I didn't know. They used some words that perfectly described situations I live with every day. I felt encouraged as I read their words which painted a picture for me. They said 'I just live my life as a different kind of normal'. They implied that rather than swim against the tide, they go with it, but tend to swim 'upside down'. I imagined lots of fish swimming together in the ocean. Yes, there was Wendy swimming along like all the others, but she was swimming upside down. Most of the other fish didn't notice. They were too busy doing what everyone else was doing. However, now and then Wendy swam into an obstacle she hadn't noticed, or swam into the path of much larger fish that threatened to gobble her up! 'Yep, that's me,' I thought. 'Just oblivious to what's going on around me!'

I so often speak without connecting to the 'sentiment' of the conversation or the 'core' expectation. I speak the words that are sparked off in my thinking or prompted to come to mind by a variety of things. These might include the words someone else is using, the interest occupying my mind at the time, or some other object of interest that passes by (e.g. birds). To be successfully involved in conversation I need to create a connection between language used, sentiment behind it and genuine interest. This can happen, but it's not normal for me to switch themes quickly. To connect with a topic that doesn't interest me, or feel comfortable with gossip or small-talk takes huge amounts of energy and attention. Therefore, for conversation to make sense, build meaning or successfully engage me, I need to be interested.

The point above is really important if we are to explore the role of conversation within the realm of autism, and if we are each going to feel comfortable using language as a tool for communication.

Language and communication

Is it normal to use only spoken language as the accepted currency for exchange of interests? It is certainly usual or normal for talkers to talk, but if you are not a 'talker' you might use other methods to converse. Some individuals might normally use silence to show their attitude towards someone or something as a way to convey their disgust, discomfort, distrust or disdain. Others might signal their opinions by using a combination of body language and silence. For example they might shrug their shoulders, throw their heads upwards or backwards and other symbolic gestures, such as walking forwards or walking away. If you are hearing-impaired you might use signing as your 'language', and this will be as normal to you as words are to talkers. For others, machines do the talking, or words are written down. For a variety of reasons, spoken language is not the only normal or usual means for communication.

Understanding one another, though, will depend upon the language we use making sense to all concerned. Within our typical society it seems that the majority rule. This means that inclusion of the wider variety of ways to converse isn't as common as it might be. Thus, those on the fringes might miss out or find themselves feeling like 'fish out of water'.

One conference I went to in South Africa was attended by people from many different backgrounds and cultures. The one thing that bound us all together was our common goal – creating a community of interest in which we all belonged. The opening 'number' at this conference was performed by several autistic children of varying ages from 5 to 15. Their common language was that of drums and dance. They were in perfect time with each other and thoroughly enjoyed the activity even though it was under bright lights and in front of more than a thousand people. These youngsters must have practised frequently, with much support and encouragement. Maybe it is the same with everyday conversations? Maybe we each need to practise the art of listening to each other and accommodating our different interests?

Currently, surrounding the AS label, there is much debate as to whether or not AS is a disability or a difference. Although in my own work I often speak about 'diffability' (being differently abled), I have always said that, as an autistic individual, I am disabled due to the non-accommodation of my difficulties. However, I also teach that AS is a particular learning style, and as such needs recognition as part of the diversely interesting world we humans occupy.

For some, autism is not seen as 'a different way of being' nor is it thought of as 'neural diversity'. It is, however, extremely handicapping and severely disabling. Rita Jordan's presentation at the above-mentioned conference (Jordan 2006) clearly acknowledged this. With her usual wisdom and professionalism, Rita summed up how autism could be either of these. In one of her slides, Rita writes under the heading of 'Alternative role of diagnosis & identification':

- Psychological definition of ASC (autistic spectrum condition).
- Medical diagnosis limited to ASD (autistic spectrum disorder).
- Both respected as part of human diversity.

Rita explained that she believes the autism spectrum could be experienced by individuals in one of two ways: as a different learning style that, when accommodated, could be thought of as an autism spectrum condition (ASC) and part of difference and neural diversity; or, if this learning style is not accommodated and catered for, the individual's condition could develop into what could be thought of as an autism spectrum disorder (ASD). Put differently, for example, Rita commented that severe autism, at times compounded by intellectual disability and sensory complications, can leave an individual deeply handicapped. If this is not recognized and appropriate supports put in place, the individual could then be experiencing a life 'disorder' which needs medical intervention.

I really appreciated this concept and can only add that, at times, AS (autism spectrum) could be thought of as ASC or ASD depending upon the individual's experience. Meaning simply that, through our lives, we can move between the two!

I am only too aware of the power of words. When one hears words like *difference* and *diversity*, one feels a sense of colour and excitement. When one hears words like *disorder* and *deviant*, one feels fear and suspicion. Rita encouraged us all to focus upon strengths and on the accommodation of ASCs so that individuals might have every opportunity to develop in a fulfilling way.

I have lots of wonderful memories of the time at the Congress in South Africa. Not only of the many, many posters of various interventions (from dietary to computer-assisted learning) and of presentations by autistic, family, professional and agency folk, but also of the community feeling that we were all in this together. Ours is a common fight for justice and understanding, with a real emphasis on uncovering individual potential and using it to the maximum. This should be part of every individual's normality. Whatever one's communication style, needs or abilities, the positive strengths should be made the most of.

So, when we take into account all of the above, if we want to be involved with successful conversation between an AS individual and one who is typical, we need to bridge the gap between us by:

- finding mutual interest as a starting point or by joining the interest of the AS individual first
- allowing the conversation to be steered by that interest to connect with ideas, concepts, hopes, and so on, so that we can build a picture of why the conversation is taking place, what it means for each individual and where we hope it may lead
- practising checking in frequently with each other so we each know we are listening, on track with one another and communicating appropriately.

Below are two examples adapted from Kluth (2003).

Interests can help to connect to new interests and conversation beyond the interest. For instance, John loves talking about the weather. Joining him at his point of interest is a typical way people interact with one another. This is often called 'small-talk'. 'Hi John, what's the weather going to do today?' 'Shall we look it up in the newspaper?' By opening the daily paper together, they can check out the weather, but they can also check out the TV programmes, the sports or some other event that could be a talking point. By being introduced to other sections of the newspaper, conversation occurs and both individuals can use this as a means to get to know one another better. Over time, John might become interested in topics beyond the weather, such as the sports section, for example. Eventually, John might show interest in sports biographies, joining a sports club or being confident to share in conversation with others.

For many individuals, conversing with someone else is easier if the attention isn't on the 'conversation' so much as it is on distribution of energies. Therefore, walking whilst talking might make conversation easier for some.

> A teacher who realized the importance of frequent movement and interaction decided to offer 'ambulatory opportunities' to all learners. He regularly gave students a prompt to discuss (e.g., What do you know about the stock market?; What is a statistic?) and then directed them to 'talk and walk' with a partner. After ten minutes of movement, he brought the students back together and asked them to discuss their conversations. (Kluth 2003, p.232)

Some individuals hear better when they are jumping on a trampoline!

Learning to be a good communicator

If we really are interested in wanting to take part in typical interaction with others, in the way that typical individuals generally do, then we need to take note of what seems to work well. In order to communicate effectively, there are certain ingredients required and when used appropriately this recipe produces a decent result. The following could be considered as a standard plan one might follow in order to converse and interact usually/typically with others.

Although this book attempts to explore concepts based around the history and foundations of, and current trends in, 'normality', it doesn't have the scope to go deeply into social skills acquisition. This short section might offer some limited ideas and support in this area, but there are lots of resources available elsewhere (see 'Useful Resources' at the end of the book). What follows is adapted with permission from Helen Glenister, Student Support Services, St Andrews University, Scotland.

Have you ever crossed the road to avoid talking to someone you recognize? Do you long to be able to go to a dinner party and converse freely with other guests? Does the phrase 'working the room' fill you with dread? Do you yearn to make more friends and influence people, but lack the courage or confidence to join all those clubs and societies? Does the thought of contributing in a tutorial, let alone delivering a 'talk', trigger an instant panic attack? Well, if you have answered 'yes' to any of the above questions, then the following might be useful to you.

The above scenarios pose some of the many challenges of social interaction, whether at college, at work or simply meeting someone whilst out. All such encounters can be handled effectively and with confidence if you have good social skills. Such skills can also go a long way to improving existing relationships with your significant others such as friends and family, whilst providing a boost to your self-esteem.

So what are social skills? In essence, social skills are little more than good communication skills or 'the art of conversation'. Here are a few tips on how to achieve this art. As with most skills, they have to be acquired through practice and perseverance.

Mastering 'small-talk'

Small-talk is the term given to non-serious, non-eventful and somewhat shallow conversations, often based around the weather, some local low-key event or some such other innocuous material. It's used to gently introduce conversation without going off into any deep subject that might be inappropriate.

Small-talk, whether we love or loathe it, is a mainstay of social interaction and invaluable as a warm-up to more serious conversations. Small-talk also acts as a useful way for us to gain an impression of someone before we give too much of ourselves away! If we lack confidence, we often make the mistake of being too open and of asking inappropriate questions in order to please the person we're speaking to, or to divert attention away from ourselves. Such tactics can be avoided through a little advanced planning, for example by having a few low-risk conversation openers to hand which are both safe and unlikely to be rebuffed.

EXERCISE 1

1. Think of one news/topical story you have heard in the last week that is of particular interest to you that you could use for small-talk. This must only be a conversational opener and not a means for you to explore your special interest, which might bore the individual you are talking with.
2. Remember one personal experience that you could use as a low-risk anecdote to get the conversation started.
3. Think of three general topics that you would wish to avoid if you were talking to strangers – and avoid talking about them. That way, you don't do further damage to your confidence!

Asking for what you want

BE POSITIVE

The attitude you adopt when making a request cannot be underestimated. If you set out with the mindset that your request will be refused, or that there is really no point, then there is none. Ever heard the phrase 'a self-fulfilling prophecy'? At the end of the day, you lose nothing by being optimistic.

SAY IT AS IT IS

Nothing is more off-putting than a request that is camouflaged in justification or apology – it only makes us suspicious. If you are not confident in what you're saying, how can anybody else be? So be concise.

KEEP OBJECTIVE

This rule needs to be applied in all interpersonal situations. *Nothing* clouds effective communication more than emotion – and not just negative emotion either. Whether deliriously happy or utterly fed up, our feelings distort our ability to make requests or communicate because they keep us locked within ourselves, thereby less able to hear what other people are saying.

KNOW THE FORM

Do your homework before the event so you know what the social etiquette is likely to be of the person or situation in which you are making the request; that is, know what level to pitch yourself at. The chances are, if you are lacking in confidence in social encounters, then you haven't grasped the finer points or the 'rules' of the game. Obviously too much deference to your boss, a professor or someone else in authority won't make you look too good in front of your mates, but making social gaffes isn't going to do you any favours either.

BE PREPARED

Not only should you ensure that you are fully conversant with your rights (if appropriate) so you avoid being side-tracked or intimidated, but be sure you really do want what you are asking for! And rehearse.

Learning to be a good listener

Learning to listen to others is not an easy task. It involves more than just noticing their words and making the right noises in their direction. Active listening means noticing body language and trying to work out the things that people leave unsaid. So what we need to do, which is what typical people normally do, is notice expressions on a person's face, what they are doing with their shoulders, hands, head and feet, as well as line these movements up with their words. For example, if an individual says 'Yes', but they shake their head from side to side, use a loud voice and walk away from you as they speak, then they probably mean 'No' or a very reluctant 'Yes'. The words alone are not enough to convey meaning. One needs to read the individual's body (language) at the same time.

It may seem an obvious point, but communication is a two-way process! And as much as we all like the sound of our own voice, hogging a conversation, due to nervousness or egotism, is not likely to impress. It is not enough, though, just to leave sufficient pauses in your monologue in order for the other person to jump in, if you then fail to hear what they are actually saying. The art of listening is a much-needed and much-lacking skill in most conversations. We all think we actually listen to our nearest and dearest, but most of us are, in truth, easily distracted by our own thoughts or something more interesting on the telly. This is why listening well is such a vital social skill to develop. Not only will it enable you to stand out from the crowd, but it is also highly seductive. Feeling heard makes us feel valued and validated.

WHAT NOT TO DO

Again, these points may seem obvious, but the next time you listen to someone (especially if you are bored) actively watch yourself, and see how many times you do any of the following:

- look at your watch
- yawn
- sigh
- look away from the person who's talking to you
- change the subject
- fidget (anything from scratching to foot tapping)
- finish other people's sentences for them (very irritating!).

WHAT YOU SHOULD DO

Actively demonstrate that you are listening by using what are termed 'minimal encouragers' such as nodding or saying 'uh-huh' and 'okay'; and make sure to:

- keep focused
- maintain good eye contact (look at their eyebrows – it gives the appearance of looking interested)
- use positive body language (don't slouch or slump; don't walk away until the conversation is finished)
- use open questions to keep the conversation going and to show your interest.

The 'Yes/No' dilemma

One of the major signs of someone who is lacking in confidence is their inability to say either yes or no appropriately. How many times, for example, do you find yourself regretting agreeing to help a friend out (again!) or 'double book' your time because you are too frightened to turn someone down?

What follows is an exercise to help you reflect on why you might find it difficult to say yes or no to particular people in specific situations. It is often when we are able to more clearly identify our feelings/behaviours around certain people that we are then able to change them (for the better!).

EXERCISE 2

First, in the table below, write down the people to whom or situations in which you find it difficult to say no. Then, in the second column, write down the reason you find it so difficult – what it is about that person or situation that would worry you if you did say no. Finally, in the third column, write down what you really think or would like to say if you didn't feel so guilt-ridden, beholden or worried. Now use those intuitive and 'rational' responses to help bolster your ability to say no, and get practising. Do the same exercise again for your problems in saying yes.

Difficulty in saying 'no'

Person / Situation	*Fear / Worry*	*True / Rational Response*
Example: Flatmate asking me out to the pub when I'm tired or need to finish an essay.	If I say no, they will be offended and won't like me any more.	I would prefer to go to the pub when I don't have so much pressure on my time and I can really relax. Perhaps I could ask my flatmate out at some later date.

Difficulty in saying 'yes'

Person / Situation	*Fear / Worry*	*True / Rational Response*
Example: Your mum has invited you out for dinner but you know she is short of money.	You will offend your mum by not going but don't want to make her overdrawn.	You accept the invite but suggest a cheap restaurant or offer to cook her dinner.

Although all of the above might seem obvious to many, to others it is a real struggle. Usual everyday activities that many of us take for granted can demand huge amounts of energy. Some individuals might not be at all interested in developing the art of conversation, but for many of us, typical or autistic, these tips might be useful.

On another note, I know when I have come home from a particular taxing social engagement just how tired I can be. This type of tiredness can last for a few days too. It's no wonder some young people after a day at school, at the office or at work come home and all they want is time to recoup. So, there are times when we may need to put our own needs for conversation and human interaction on hold and give others the space they need.

CHAPTER 5

Knowing Our Minds, Knowing Our Rights

Knowing one another

There are many different sayings about mind. The following are a few examples:

- 'What's on your mind?'
- Mind over matter.
- Know your own mind.
- 'Mind your own business.'
- 'Mind this for me.'
- 'Do you mind?'
- Being mindful.

So often in so many relationships people expect that the other person will be able to 'read' their mind and just 'know' what it is they are thinking, wanting or needing. Unfortunately for the individual who has this expectation the other party may not be aware of or privy to this information. This can then cause a multitude of difficulties. For example, a wife may expect that her husband 'knows' that she needs him to listen to her and to stop reading his newspaper. But in reality the husband may not realize this. The wife might then become upset but not share this fact with her husband. Eventually the husband might think that his wife seems a bit hostile, concluding that she is tired or that she needs some space. So, he might decide that the best thing to do is go outside and tidy up his shed. His wife might take this as rejection and think that her husband is being thoughtless and insensitive to her needs. When, actually, he simply wasn't aware of them. If this couple doesn't communicate about what each is thinking, then the relationship might suffer as a consequence. Yet over and over again in so many situations individuals just expect the other person will read their minds. No one reads minds! What some people do is read 'the signs'. We need to check in often and talk to each other so we can be available to what is happening for one another. If the other person chooses not to share what is 'on their mind', then we may need to stay available, be a friend but not pressure them.

When one is asked the question 'What's on your mind?', this isn't the same as being asked 'Of what mind are you?' or 'What do you think?' They sound like the same question, but they are different. So what is the usual or normal way individuals pose these sorts of questions? There might not be a regular way, so much as regular sets of circumstances that set the scene for the question. It's this bit of information that we might miss if we are an AS individual.

Unfortunately, such questions imply that one has an understanding and can immediately access one's thoughts in context with the background of the question. Making up one's own mind about a particular thing and relating this in context are two different things and, as autistic individuals, we may not always connect things in a way that makes sense or is in contact with the other person's interest.

What I have observed is that sometimes individuals give responses that are not what they are thinking at all. Rather, it might be the answer they think someone wants from them. As well as being connected to the wider interests of those concerned to appreciate another's mind on a topic, one needs to get to know them as individuals. Sometimes people might wear a mask to cover up their real feelings. Especially if they don't feel safe, feel insecure, feel embarrassed or are trying to be polite. This type of mask isn't an actual physical mask but rather one constructed from an adopted stance. For example, one might say 'Yes please' to accepting a cup of coffee whilst visiting with a friend, but not really want the coffee. They do this to be polite.

It takes courage and conviction to have a mind of one's own, especially if it differs from typical expectations, thinking or viewpoints.

Some individuals might not know that what they are thinking is constructed from ideas they have been fed. It's quite difficult to know one's own mind and separate it from the communal thought or expectation of others.

Knowing one's own mind or thoughts about something can be extra tricky when feeling unsure or 'torn' between certain viewpoints, or simply not having had sufficient time to process the information well enough to know one's answer. Processing time for thinking, problem solving or weighing up one's thoughts and feelings to build a connection and activate an understanding can take some of us longer than it does others. I'm an 'instant' kind of person who tends towards snap decisions. I don't always take enough time to think things through and process them well enough. This means I may speak without evaluating whether or not my words are needed, necessary, appropriate or welcome! I also have found it difficult to accommodate situations where others have changed their minds about something they previously agreed to. This might have happened because as they have processed the information they have come to realize it's not what they want.

It is normal and usual to recognize that individuals have a right to their own minds and own points of view; this is a given. But how often does this really happen? More often than not people are offended when others do not agree with their view or taste or idea. It isn't easy appreciating that someone might not like the things we like, might not agree with our decisions or might not value the things we value. I know sometimes I find it hard to understand my partner doesn't like marmalade, and she finds it hard to understand I don't like garlic!

This might seem like a trivial thing, but it actually can bear upon wider issues. We all have rights. But are these always equal? The right to a normal life and a normal amount of respect for one's views is legitimate. If, however, I find it hard to know my own mind, or if I find it hard to understand the mind of others, it will mean everyday life will be prone to processing difficulties, leading to miscommunication, misunderstanding and misconceptions. In autism this seems normal for me! I know we each have a right to be understood. The difficulty might be arriving at the same understanding. I have already suggested that it might be easier for autistic individuals to relate once others join their interest (see Chapter 2) and use it to help take us into other areas that need attention.

Rights

The sections above explain the idea of mind as a system of interests. One has a mind of one's own and others have their own minds too. Communication between us can be difficult for all sorts of reasons. However, the idea that one has 'rights' and that it's okay to have them is often obscured by belief systems, such as 'What is normal?' Sometimes it's in one's interests or the interests of others to 'rob' individuals of rights. At other times we can grow up believing that our rights are not equal to those of others due to our status in life. So, within the typical and usual concepts of normal, 'rights' are given to certain individuals deemed as 'being worthy'. This might mean those 'in authority' or seen as being 'the authority'. Unfortunately this perceived 'power' often prevents potent questions being asked because those of us not 'in authority' don't believe or feel that we have 'the right' to question those in power over us. This affects families and society as a whole in many different ways. It may impact negatively upon the type of education children are able to access, the types of friendships one is encouraged to develop, clubs one might join, clothing one 'should' wear, music one should listen to, or the ways one interacts with and treats fellow human beings.

Some individuals are deemed as not being as worthy of rights as others due to their responses not being considered normal. For example, language is considered the traditional normal currency of communication. Therefore, if you don't use language as your communication tool, you may be considered disabled, disordered or dysfunctional. Talkers in modern society feel uncomfortable with non-talkers and, to help themselves feel comfortable again, they might finish a sentence for the other individual, put what they think the individual is wanting into words for them, or even totally disregard the non-talking individual as someone who doesn't 'have anything to say'. The idea that communication might be presented in non-verbal terms (such as signs, pictures, facilitated communicating, artificial intelligence, etc.) is often not considered, or only considered as communication of a lesser credibility. Yet, each and every individual has a right to communicate their thoughts, desires, needs, and so on. This applies equally to talkers and to non-talkers.

When it comes to being informed about one's own health, one is often considered as the last person who needs to know: 'Oh, the doctor knows best, dear.' I have often wondered about this statement. Why is it used? What does the doctor know that is best? Does this mean it is normal for a doctor to know things about the patient, but not tell the patient? Is the idea of 'best' meant to apply to the patient or to the doctor? As human beings of equal status, I suggest we also have a right to know and to decide what is 'best' for us. If for some reason this is inappropriate (due to age, illness, diminished capacity, etc.) then one needs to have a 'trusted other' that information can be shared with. This enables decisions to be made that we can rest assured will be in our best interest. Of course, finding a 'trusted other' isn't always easy and needs to be done with care. Making sure our interests are uppermost in this situation might mean signing statutory declaration forms, having 'a living will' or giving power of attorney with regards to general, medical or financial matters to a family member, reliable friend or a solicitor.

CHAPTER 6

Autism, Sexuality and Normal

This book would be incomplete if it didn't mention sexuality. As well as looking at issues of human 'rights', needs and education, some of the experiences AS individuals report concerning autism and sexuality are at the very heart of what it means to be normal.

I have heard it said that autistic individuals may not be interested in sex because they don't do relationships. Well, I have to disagree with these sentiments! We have seen that AS is a spectrum of differing characteristics and experiences that change over time. This is one reason why it is located on Axis I and not on Axis II in the *Diagnostic and Statistical Manual of Mental Disorders* (Axis I is for conditions that improve and change over time, while Axis II is for those that do not). Therefore, even if an autistic individual doesn't display interest in age-appropriate relationships as a child, it does not mean they will stay that way as they grow up.

Just like the rest of humanity autistic individuals have genetic predispositions and personality traits. However, the package we are today is also influenced by our insights, learning styles, education, culture, gender and even autonomy levels. According to Dinah Murray (personal communication, 2002):

> ...we may be less likely (or more likely if insights cause obsessive grief/depression to dominate our thinking) to need to conform and more 'free' (or less, as the case may be) to behave in accordance with our dispositions and/or desires. Perhaps conflict in our sexuality arises once we become 'aware' and it actually matters to us what others think? Or/and conflict arises for us when our own autonomy is ruptured or weak and we can't locate any way to boost it?

Because being monotropic (single-minded, led by an interest system that is single-focused) might be a feature of autism, this could mean that either one's thinking or feeling states, rather than being disseminated across both, might occupy all of one's attention. So, if, for example, feelings dominate thinking, it becomes very difficult to switch off from what one is switched on to! This will apply to all areas of one's life and learning, including sexuality.

The sexuality spectrum

Sexuality will mean different things to different people. Usually it is thought of as a coalition of human gender equipment, sensuality, sexual maturity and sexual needs. However, I don't think it is always this 'black and white'.

Jim Sinclair, an autistic individual who sees himself as asexual says:

> It is hearing that because I have no sexual feelings, I have no feelings; that because I do not feel love in my groin, I cannot feel love at all. I define myself as asexual, because if I am asexual I have all the equipment I need. I define my expressions of sensuality, eros, and love as nonsexual, because if they are nonsexual they are not rendered invalid by my asexuality. I define my love as authentic, because I define my humanity as complete and unimpaired. (Sinclair 1987)

Maybe there are other AS individuals, like myself, who tend towards monotropism in their sexuality. In so many things we are all-or-nothing people, so this might apply to sexuality too. I know individuals who say they don't think of themselves as 'sexual', do not experience sexual desire, do not masturbate or even have sexual fantasies. I also know other AS individuals who say they are very sexual and need to express their sexuality in practical terms. This might mean taking care of their sexual needs themselves, or it might mean sharing in sexual activity with others. Wherever an individual is on the sexuality spectrum, their needs, legitimate preferences and disposition should be respected.

In my own experience (which I write about in *Sex, Sexuality and the Autism Spectrum*, Jessica Kingsley Publishers, 2004), I have always felt more 'at home' with the male gender expectations of society, than the female. For many, many years I pondered about becoming 'male' and felt literally that I had been assigned the wrong gender. I just didn't 'feel' female. Now I recognize that societal engineered 'feelings' that are supposed to accompany 'femininity' are constructed and promoted rather than 'actual' for many females. Therefore, my branch of 'femaleness' is fine! I can still be 'female' yet feel more at home in masculine expectations (dress, emotional response, academia, etc.).

With regard to sexual orientation and autism, I'd like to know what the statistics are. Maybe sexuality and autism are not so clearly defined by gender as in the typical population? I tend to think, anecdotally, that there are proportionally more homosexual, bisexual and transgender individuals in the AS population than in the typical population because we are not so aware of or concerned with societal expectation. We don't swim with the tide!

Accessing appropriate sex education and practical support hasn't been very easy for AS individuals. Maybe this has meant that discovering normal or appropriate sexuality has seemed out of reach for many.

To access education, information and understanding one must know that this is what one needs. Then one might need support in finding ways to search out that information. Being informed should mean one is equipped with understanding that translates to practical application. In AS, however, this might not happen simply because one isn't aware. Initially just 'knowing you don't know' can be difficult to sort out. But does this make us less normal, or might it mean one is 'in the dark' a while longer than most?

If, as suggested above, monotropism in autism means being singly focused and more often than not occupied by one interest above all others, then 'feeling' may rule above 'thinking' or vice versa, and we tend to be dominated by which is the stronger of the two. Hormones tend to charge one's emotional state, and in the context of sexuality, this will mean sexual expression is not always carefully thought out. If you don't know the difference between public and private, and if you are not self-aware, let alone aware of others, sexual behaviour might express itself as a 'natural' part of self without due regard to or respect for one's environment.

This is not done to shock or embarrass anyone. For example, at the extreme end of a sexual spectrum there might be individuals who will masturbate in public, might use inappropriate objects for sexual release, stalk objects of sexual desire, fail to understand appropriate sexual behaviour and, in general, might be 'ruled' by sexual obsession. Whilst at the other end others may simply not understand the everyday stuff of personal hygiene, monthly menstruation, relationships, issues of public and private, and so on. It would be tempting to see this whole arena of sexuality in AS as 'too hard' and avoid the subject; but avoiding it won't make it go away or diminish its power.

We need to move policy into practice. This will mean taking each individual and profiling their needs. After all, being a sexual being, wherever one fits on the 'sexuality' continuum, is normal. First, we must accept and respect individuals as individuals and recognize their individuality. Second, assess where they are on the sexuality continuum, so we can pinpoint the issues they need support with. Third, put it all together into a plan of intervention, education or practical support, according to what we find.

Other issues to consider

Sensory profiling

As stated previously, sensory modalities in typical development are interconnected and interrelated. This might not be the case in AS, where our senses sometimes become quickly overloaded. For example, we might have difficulties with the sound of someone's voice, the way they smell (perfume, deodorant), how they feel to touch, how our own bodies 'feel' when touched, the sight of body parts, and the sensations of stimulation. I wonder if this is usual or typical for other individuals too, but no one ever talks about it?

When it comes to affection and intimacy some of us are quickly overstimulated and cannot bear to be kissed for very long, touched in certain ways or places (nipples, legs, face), cope with close proximity of another person, or even cope with the way we feel when undressed. Others may be in a state of under-arousal and find they cannot respond sexually without strong, deep, long and in-depth stirring of sensual contact, imagery, physical contact and/or a long build-up to sexual expression.

It is very important in any consideration of sexual matters in AS that sensory profiling is considered. I think this is also a consideration in typical relationships, but because of the expectation upon typical individuals to be a particular way they are cheated out of the opportunities to own their difficulties. For example, a man is expected to perform sexually in a particular way to be considered a good lover. If he has difficulties in this area, he might mask them rather than admit to them because of the stigma attached to concepts of maleness embedded in sexual performance.

Intellect and communication style

Just like it is important to consider sensory needs in connection to sexuality it is also important to consider intellectual and communications style. It might seem obvious that intellect needs to play a part in how information is presented and processed. However, some AS individuals, even if they can identify what their concerns and needs are, don't use spoken language to relate these concerns to others. Therefore, it is not unusual to assume AS individuals who don't talk and are not deaf must be intellectually disabled (ID). However, this might not be the case at all. Rather, it might be that spoken language is not their preferred form of communication or is not accessible as a form of communication, or doesn't appear to them to be a necessary form of communication. If an AS individual does have ID, then information needs to be presented at a level and in a format that they can process and apply to their lives.

Role-play

I think that when it comes to relating to anyone at any level, role-play can be useful. As in many areas, AS individuals have difficulty learning when they are only *told* something, rather than having practical, hands-on, demonstrations. Role-playing how to meet other people, how to talk to them and how to deal with problems that occur is an important part of learning about relationships and sexuality. Role-playing helps to make some of the more obscure concepts easier to understand and utilize. Although normal interaction in social settings is assumed to be understood by so many, it isn't always as obvious as it seems. Typical 'modelling' behaviours often take place in typical families. But for many of us who are not typical or who don't get the opportunity to model after some significant 'other', role-play and even game-playing on the computer can be useful options (Ryokai, Vaucelle and Cassell 2003).

For AS individuals technology could be the greatest tool that helps unlock the mysteries of sexuality, relationships and communication. Role-play via technology also assists and accommodates monotropic learning styles. Computer animation (depicting 'roles', rules and rituals), especially when interactive and 'alive' with meaning, may help to build connection. The type of connection typical individuals learn quite readily might be less accessible for us to learn traditionally. The issues outlined above could assist with the developing of a quality of life for us that should be every individual's 'right'. (See 'Useful Resources' at the end of the book for more information.)

CHAPTER 7

Whose Normal Is It Anyway?

By Dinah Murray

Autism is by definition a condition in which society plays a role (see Chapter 2); some aspects of what that role is are considered in this chapter. Using several of the 'signs of autism spectrum' adapted from a website list intended to help people recognize autism, I show how little translation they require in order equally to be applied to non-autistic behaviour. This will make it explicit how the value judgements involved depend on one's point of view. I suggest that inappropriate behaviours perpetuated by Others contribute to the social climate which turns autistic spectrum conditions into disorders (Jordan 2007; and see Wendy's discussion in Chapter 4).

All the 'inappropriate behaviours' of which young autistic people are accused are mirrored by adults on the typical side, who inflict them upon the young autistic people as they grow up: non-communication; repetitive behaviours; obsessions with alien topics; failure to appreciate distinct points of view; insensitivity to personal space; etc. If Others can learn to recognize when they are producing harmful behaviours such as those discussed below, then fewer 'crises of disorder' will happen to autistic people. As a result, their (as well as the Others') abilities will be maximized rather than suppressed.

Extreme difficulty in learning language

It is hard to learn another's language unless it is being used to express meaning in a shared context. Spoken language needs to relate to common interests if it is to be effective communication. Likewise, tuning into another person's interests gives one a chance to learn their language. Others typically stop doing this once a child has acquired a basic vocabulary. Instead they begin using the acquired words invasively and directively.

People routinely seek to get children involuntarily involved in externally imposed would-be common interests. They expect children to disengage from their own current interests and move willingly into the imposed spheres of interest. In fact this is a key dynamic of social life – language reaches, arouses and informs other people's interests and, as a result, people become involved with each other's projects and enter into many shifting communities of interest.

Keeping up with the flux of normal social discourse involves a capacity to switch topics comfortably. People with deep interests may be so absorbed in each current interest that this rapid switching is deeply uncomfortable or impossible to adjust to. Much of the difficulty for autistic children and adults in learning verbal language may be attributed to failure on the part of Others to tune in and make them comfortable with the speech offered them by using it to address what they are interested in. Similarly, Others may fail to allow enough processing time to adjust to a necessary change of topic.

Others' failure to note and adjust to where the autistic interests are guarantees that their every attempt to communicate on the autistic person's own terms is doomed. They thus deprive themselves of learning the autistic person's language. It is tuning in to another's interests that provides the chance to learn *their* meanings. Many non-autistic people also have extreme difficulty in picking up autistic people's non-verbal language and may take years longer than another autistic person would to tune in successfully (see the YouTube video 'In My Language' for a powerful statement about non-verbal language and meaning: Baggs 2006b).

Here is Amanda Baggs, a young woman with autism, writing about how someone – another autistic person – eventually used words successfully to communicate with her:

> ...she used language in a way I understood. She used it based on a context that she could perceive that most people could not. A context close enough to what I perceived to make it work...

> One thing that helped a lot was communication with me. Most people before that did not communicate with me. They communicated *at* me. They either were telling me what to do, or attempting to hold a conversation with something that from what I could tell was three feet away from me, or inside their own heads, and nothing to do with me at all. I was stunned that someone was talking to me instead of to all kinds of hallucinations in their minds that were not really there, and getting to know me instead of telling me what to do. (Baggs 2006c)

Inappropriate response to people, and invading Others' personal space

Others typically shun autistics, mock them, or try to fix them. Even the most well meaning tend to address autistics as though from a superior position, which confers the right to instruct and direct them. They generally attempt to invade autistic personal space with vigour, determination and an air of righteousness, and they use speech to attempt to dominate thought processes. They invade autistic space by forcing eye contact, by preventing chosen movements such as flapping, rocking or other behaviours currently judged inappropriate by the majority.

Some Others weep and moan and deplore their autistic child's existence; they wallow in self-pity and congratulate each other on admitting how Truly Dreadful it all is. They exchange sympathetic talk about considering murdering their children (see Thierry and Solomon 2006) – or at least normalizing them at any cost (cost to be borne by the health/insurance system if possible). They describe their plight and that of their families as 'The worst thing that can happen to a family'.

This culture of non-acceptance is very harmful to autistic people, leading to their alienation, exclusion, persecution and even murder (see Smith 2007). And what, one wonders, may be the effect on the developing psyche of hearing oneself discussed in this way?

In my view, all the behaviours just described are at least as inappropriate as anything produced by an autistic child who is still trying to figure out 'What's going on?' and 'What are the rules?'

Given the above, is it inappropriate or even surprising if children with autism avoid eye contact, resist being picked up or cuddled, and seem to tune out of the world? In addition to all those possible reasons for social avoidance, autistics of all ages may have particular sensitivities to sensory experience which make them aversive, for example, to certain ways of being touched or to the intensity of eye contact. They may be terrified by the suddenness of the rude Other breaking into their attention tunnel and subjecting them to strange feelings – and sometimes doing this again and again in spite of distressed autistic reactions which should be obvious to the Other.

Others may be unbearably noisy – and as the autistics try to block them out, Others may also tend to get louder and louder in trying to get their attention, thus violently attempting to invade the child's auditory space.

Then again, there are Others who tune autistics right out of their world and see them, if at all, as aliens. Mostly Others avoid looking at or engaging in any way with people whose behaviours they find odd, unless they are trying to change them – or perhaps treating them as theatre.

So to sum up, Others tend either to avoid eye contact completely or to impose it inappropriately. They also generally fail to tune in to autistic interests and therefore do not notice or make any attempt to understand autistic meanings.

Inability or reduced ability to play cooperatively with other children or to make friends

Non-autistic children appear to have a reduced ability to accept children who won't be bossed about, or who find make-believe games puzzling or alarming. They need special training to help them recognize how to cooperate successfully with autistic children instead of being annoyed or alienated by them. Others need to learn to give autistic children time, and show them clearly what is the current potential fun. Research has demonstrated that autistic children are happy to join in and imitate their peers when the social context is simplified for them and the means of imitating the Other are obvious (Field *et al.* 2001).

Tendency to form obsessions and perform repetitive actions

'Restricted' interests are in the diagnostic criteria for autism. The model of mind as an interest system which Wendy and I are using in this book is based on my PhD thesis (Murray 1986) and was further extensively developed in collaboration with Mike Lesser (see Lesser and Murray 1998). In Murray *et al.* (2005) we showed how the monotropism idea first discussed publicly in 1992 could underlie all the diagnostic criteria for autism. According to this idea, autistic children are specially inclined to give their full attention to what they're doing – just so long as the task is where their interest is, not imposed from without.

Rather than having lots of rather diluted mild interests constantly a bit aroused, autistic children and adults tend to have powerful, wholly absorbing ones that arise from within themselves in relation to what they are personally drawn to. Because their interests are often so much less deeply felt, Others can change direction very lightly and easily and tend to expect everyone to be equally fickle. Since the wholly absorbing interest may also occupy an unusually large proportion of the autistic individual's time and processing resources, and will not be easily displaced, it may attract the 'obsession' label – perhaps especially if it is not socially approved.

However, Others do tend to have strong *social* priorities, which show themselves as persistent interests in matters concerning presentation of self and judgements of the acceptability or otherwise of behaviour. Those priorities are embedded within a much larger discourse, which sustains and reinforces them. Some people, caught in this social trap, seem to the more autistic of us to be able to see nothing outside a very limited set of issues, which they become obsessed with fixing. That is, these issues occupy a very large proportion of their time and their processing resources, leaving these Others unable to see positive aspects of their situation. This inability can be harmful for all concerned, causing repetitive behaviours and utterances that make no sense to the autistic observer.

Need for a rigid, highly structured routine

It is often noted that autistic children need to take part in their own structured routines. This would not be noteworthy, since everybody likes to do that – ask yourself about your own life and what it's like to have your expectations thwarted. The problem may be that these children tend to have unusual routines – routines not modelled on Others' routines, or which have no obvious purpose to Others. Once again, Others' failure to understand autistic minds, and their inability to accept non-imitative behaviour as worthwhile or meaningful, can have a strongly negative impact on communication, cooperation and motivation.

What is more, Others too will tend to have their own rigid, highly structured routines. An example from a school environment: 'When the bell rings you must stand up and leave the room; before the bell rings you must stay sitting, be silent unless spoken to, and not leave the room.' This is confusing and un-obvious, and yet Others will become furious and show every sign of distress when these routines are not rigidly adhered to.

People of all sorts truly do *start* life preferring to avoid trouble if they know how, but Others do not always explain the rules very clearly. Much autistic frustration may arise from attempting to follow the rules as far as one understands them, without having had them properly explained or defined.

Others appear generally to be content with high levels of blurriness and uncertainty, in exchange for the comfort of doing what everybody else is doing. That comfort is no protection against the icy blasts of inconsistency and contradiction that can so trouble the autistic child or adult, yet go unnoticed by Others. We shall return below to examine more closely this defective response to inconsistency in the majority of Others.

Inability to understand other people's feelings

To illustrate how problematic Others' understanding of autistic feelings can be, here is Amanda Baggs again, this time being reminded

> of the time I came in while we were picking someone up from a day program that took place at an institution (she and I were both clients of the same agency, and that agency often doubled up on rides). I hadn't realized it was a live-in institution until we got inside, and I was visibly jumpy I guess. The woman we'd come to pick up was crying. This made me even jumpier, because I thought she might get punished for crying. So I was sitting there afraid of the staff, and all the staff rushed to reassure me that there was nothing scary about *the woman who was crying.* (Baggs 2006a)

Others may need special training before they are capable of overcoming their inability to understand autistic feelings. For example, they may benefit from social skills training specifically targeted at this deficit. They are likely to need help in 'reading' non-standard expressions of emotion and picking up on communications before the frustrations of not being understood boil over and reduce still further the chances of mutual understanding.

Frequent crying and tantrums for no apparent reason

Others exhibit these behaviours constantly. For example, somebody flaps a bit, spins a bit, rocks a bit – and the Other repeatedly physically intervenes. When the action is renewed again, the Other may start to shout repeatedly, saying the same sorts of thing over and over again, or even to shriek and scream uncontrollably.

Some Others also cry a lot while talking or writing about their autistic children – and they may do so right in front of the children. Others may burst into tears again and again while railing against behaviours the autistic little person sees and feels as completely harmless and agreeable. Others may even phone a friend for affirmation of the horrors they share, conversation in which both Others can be heard by their children expressing their autism-hostile views.

I recently heard an unnamed woman on the television summing up what may be a universal truth about human beings: 'What do we all care about most? – getting the affirmation that you're doing the best you can...'

Those parents who are busily seeking such affirmation for themselves from each other are not registering the fact they are denying such affirmation to their children. For a penetrating account of the harm done to autistic children by this sort of attitude and behaviour, please see Jim Sinclair's eloquent text 'Don't mourn for us' (Sinclair 1993).

Some autism charities raise funds by talking about plagues, epidemics, and cancers, or quoting unhappy parents like James Watson of DNA fame who says 'nothing worse [than autism] can happen to a family' (Autism Speaks 2006). Yet, even on a website such as Autism Speaks, some Others, who rejoice in their autistic children's goodwill, have started a thread. One posted about the joy of her moment of acceptance: 'When I finally prayed to God not to change my child but to change me so I could help my child.'

All the contributors to the Posautive YouTube group (which I own) repudiate the attitude of mourning and despair which can so corrupt Others' capacity to cooperate and communicate constructively. It appears that this attitude change may occur in almost anyone who uses direct observation rather than relying on received opinion.

Inappropriate or absent emotional responses

Given the points we have been discussing, it is likely that Others are unaware of much autistic emotional responding, only noticing it when it disturbs their peace of mind.

It is also the case that some autistic people report control issues in this area, and are unable to adjust their facial expressions to fit social expectations, even when they have grown up and become increasingly aware of those expectations. There are many personal reports of autistic people smiling or laughing uncontrollably in response to being horrified; they have no intention to offend, and they are feeling very bad in themselves at such times (Lawson 2006). In these cases, Others have strong cultural expectations which they can have great difficulty setting aside, and which may provoke inappropriate anger or disgust in them. Here the autistic emotional response is appropriate but its outward appearance is not adjusted to be socially meaningful, while the Others' inappropriately hostile emotional responses are insensitive and even deliberately hurtful.

Once again, Others may need some training to help them avoid these alienating behaviours by better understanding what's going on for the autistic person – an area in which Others are typically mind-blind, though that is not necessarily a lifelong feature of their condition.

Apart from the differences of presentation just discussed, there is also a self-reported difference in the general quality of emotional response. Sometimes this is referred to as being 'emotionally flat', sometimes as being 'uninvolved', 'just an observer', 'behind glass' (Lawson), life as a video, etc. You can hear Elizabeth Culling and her partner Paul, who are soon to be married, talking about emotion on YouTube as part of the National Autistic Society's Think Differently Campaign (Wady and Culling 2007). Elizabeth says 'I describe myself as being emotionally flat' and finds this in many ways a satisfactory and sometimes rewarding way to be.

Yet it is clearly not quite as simple as that. For one thing, there is research to show autistic people who are able to speak, and therefore in principle able to self-report, experience the same emotional reactions viscerally, but without the reactions having an impact on what they say or perhaps on what they think (Shalom *et al.* 2006). For another thing, what about excitement? Anger? Curiosity? Enthusiasm? Fear? These are all emotions which I have often seen displayed, usually with intensity, by people on the autism spectrum.

I propose that emotions can helpfully be divided into three levels of activity for the purposes of clarifying some of the reported differences between autistic and Other emotional experience:

1. Observer's emotions.
2. Participant's emotions.
3. Para-participant's emotions.

Observer's emotions

At the most basic level I place 'observer's emotions' – those arising from non-active engagement with the world, including forming a judgement about what's going on, curiosity, desire to understand, find out and discover ('pure' interest).

I label these confidently as emotions mainly because they are experienced more or less intensely, like any other emotion (a view supported by the well-known work of Plutchik (1962, 1982)).

Truth is the object of most of these observer emotions, and their satisfaction consists in certainty. According to Dewey: 'The quest for certainty is a quest for peace which is assured, an object which is unqualified by risk and the shadow of fear which action casts' (Dewey 1929, p.12). Dewey argued that certainty was a human need, an essential basis for the courage needed to repeatedly overcome the fear of action. Unresolved issues are as psychologically potent as any other passions – they drive cognitive action until satisfaction is achieved. These are the emotions that initiate cognition.

Simple wonder, another observer viewpoint but without active concern for understanding, is the remaining Level 1 emotion. In this model of emotions, wonder is the only emotional state that imposes no personal or social meaning. Even truth-seeking has an agenda. Wonder has no agenda (there is nothing to be acted upon).

Participant's emotions

Aversion/attraction, fear, anger, hope, enthusiasm, despair, sorrow, boredom, love, hate, joy, frustration and fulfilment – these are the emotions that

- initiate action and therefore involve risk
- have a direction towards the future and a relationship with the past
- have direction beyond perception and affect, and are affected by expectations
- can create multiple and potentially conflicting agendas
- direct observation, and determine what aspects of a situation are noticed.

Level 2 emotions belong primarily to the living of life, to the people taking part in its drama, rather than to any audience or witness there may be. As shared emotions they are often attached to shared purposes and outcomes; it is a self-evident truth that people performing tasks together cooperate most effectively when in emotional harmony. Occasions for sharing Level 2 emotions face to face are surely much rarer in the 21st century than ever before.

Autistic single-mindedness may mean that Level 1 and Level 2 emotions will tend not to occur simultaneously for an autistic person: they may either be observing or participating in what they do, not both at once. The exception is of course when the desire to know yields that beautiful synthesis of curiosity and action that leads to experiment and discovery.

Para-participant's emotions

These include any Level 2 emotions *experienced from an observer's point of view*, plus some which themselves imply the involvement of Others: embarrassment, approval, pride, scorn, derision, shame and envy.

Other people's judgements can directly determine the nature of these emotions. Because these have an observer's point of view – the observer becomes the audience – they can completely replace Level 1 emotions. These emotions can override the desire for truth, and the values they imply can override truth values. Since they do not require real participation, with its inevitable risks, they need not cause real suffering, and they can subsist at a low level at the same time as other emotions.

Level 3 emotions presumably relate to the development of theatrical imagination that I have noted elsewhere (Murray 2000). They may be a particularly prominent feature of late 20th- and early 21st-century life, as more and more of life is led second-hand and at the same time more and more attention is devoted to passing fashions.

These Level 3 emotions are likely to be the least accessible to autistic thinking, since they incorporate Others' attitudes. Their propensity to co-exist with a range of other emotions may also be problematic given the autistic preference for single-mindedness. In contrast, Others appear to find it difficult or impossible not to prioritize Other-oriented values (see Lawson 2001).

In line with Michelle Dawson's proposal (in Mottron *et al.* 2006) that higher-order processing is optional for autistic thinkers and obligatory for Others, I propose it is only with effort and unusual focus that Others can keep Level 3 feelings out of their cognitive processes.

Overall, as Mitchell *et al.* (2007) demonstrate, emotions use processing resources. Therefore, having many emotions aroused at the same time means reduced resources available and hence reduced intensity of feeling. The monotropic strategy of concentrating processing resources rather than spreading them thin may produce a smaller range of stronger feelings than Others typically experience.

When autistic people describe themselves as emotionally flat, or seeing life as a video (Lawson 2000), they may be describing their most typical pattern of emotional engagement at Level 1: watching and noting, and doing so with greater accuracy than Others do (Mottron *et al.* 2006), perhaps because they are not feeling the pull of all those other concerns and desires to please. They are 'merely observing', which Others find so hard. This is the emotional state behind the scientific attitude that Marc Segar (1997) singles out as a key identifying feature of autistic ways of thinking. It abhors inaccuracy and contradiction.

Autistic people may also be atypical in more frequently experiencing simple wonder, as discussed above, if our premise about autistic single-mindedness is correct.

I suggest the other most typical pattern of emotional arousal found in autism is wholehearted engagement at Level 2 in actions of some sort, without regard to risk or opinion. It is possible that there may be a spontaneous oscillation between Level 1 and Level 2 basic states. In contrast, Others can have all the emotion boxes lit at once and be unable to turn them off.

It is also likely that emotional awareness at Level 3 becomes accessible to many or most autistic people as well as Others, as they grow up. It just may take usefully longer if you're autistic, ensuring that access to these complex and mixable emotions is only acquired when personal cognitive strategies are already firmly in place. Therefore, for autistic people, all experience is not inescapably placed within the social sphere and warped by the social prism.

In my view, this extract from Gerard Manley Hopkins' poem 'God's Grandeur' (written in the 19th century but not published till 1918) summarizes this difference from a poet's standpoint:

Generations have trod, have trod, have trod;
And all is seared with trade; bleared, smeared with toil;
And wears man's smudge and shares man's smell: the soil
Is bare now, nor can foot feel, being shod.

And for all this, nature is never spent...

In the market place, Level 3 emotions rule, and the capacity to model Other minds is an imperative. But having a different type of emotional distribution and commitment does not equate to not having emotions.

When attempting to embrace points of view beyond their own, Others may need to be trained in identifying and adapting to emotional patterns that attach more importance to accuracy than theirs do, or that may be engaged with the pursuit of unfamiliar goals.

The attitudes encapsulated at Level 3 are enmeshed with Others' judgements, and so they may not be easily dislodged. However, a more enlightened take on autistic points of view, and a more tolerant take on what to disapprove of, greatly reduces the mismatch between these contrasting emotional styles.

The culturally relative value judgements of Level 3 emotionality currently inform both the diagnostic criteria for autism and the assumption that a certain limited way to be normal is The Right Way. It is hoped this book will demonstrate that such a view is distorted, detrimental to both autistics and Others, and just plain wrong.

Acknowledgements

I want to thank Wendy first, for being who she is, and for encouraging me to write this chapter. Next I owe a big thanks to Selina Postgate who ran a sharp editorial eye over this for me, much improving it in the process. And I owe thanks to all the many autistic people who've helped me gain a less prejudiced view of autism myself; in relation to this particular piece the early work of the Institute for the Study of Neuro-Typicality (ISNT) was surely influential. Thank you everyone.

CHAPTER 8

Inclusion and Understanding

Inclusion as normality

I have always been in favour of inclusion. That is to say, I am against 'exclusion' when it means outlawing or separating some individuals from others, forcibly and against their will. I agree with Jim Sinclair, who is also autistic, when he writes:

> I do not know of any advocate from within the disability community who believes that inclusion should not be an available option. Disability advocates believe that disabled people should be able to go anywhere and do anything in mainstream society. Among disabled people, even the strongest critics of inclusion would probably object to school districts and other community institutions being permitted to exclude or segregate people who wish to be included. Inclusion MUST be an available option for those who choose it. (Sinclair 1998)

However, the very term that defines me as an individual with autism states that I am disabled due to deficits in three areas of functioning: social understanding, communication and imagination. My experience as a human being raises the question: 'Are there not many individuals, with or without autism, who have these difficulties?' Even the 'cool, confident kids' who make it into all manner of successful adult pursuits must, for example, fit somewhere into the adult statistics of the one in three divorce rates in our Western society.

So, even though it might be easier to feel 'included' for any student at school who is 'cool', attractive and confident, lots of ordinary individuals, let alone students with a disability like AS, really struggle to find where they fit in today's society.

Creative strategies

Sometimes children and adults find 'fitting in' very difficult. Maybe we are unsure of protocol or are just not sure of what to say or how to go about it. Sometimes individuals are not keen on the activity or just don't see the point. For individuals who appear not to be skilled or confident, it's much harder to join in with group activity. The other side to this is that the group itself might pick up on this discomfort and, as a consequence, they might appear to 'reject' the individual concerned. For example, at school a child might not be chosen by others to join in their team for sports activities; or a child might be ostracized by other children not choosing to sit near them or play with them. If, however, the particular difficulties had been understood and had been accommodated, many childhood experiences of school might have been different: for example, a smart teacher could give a child a role that facilitates inclusion. If other children are given a reason to include a child they are more likely to respect that child. There are many other things that children with disabilities might be able to do other than join in with the team sports; for example, being allowed to keep score during ball games, or to design the rules for a game and teach the other children how to play that game.

Understanding the social rules of any group and knowing how to implement them is crucial to inclusion. But understanding how these change and teaching adaptability to 'difference' are also crucial to inclusion. Inclusion in education, as an ideal, could be a reality for many during school years, if difference was fostered as part of being normal.

It's interesting that at school, if you are autistic, you are encouraged to put away your 'interest' and move between your own interest and that of the group or of other individuals. However, at university this concept is often changed; you are encouraged to 'specialize' and focus on a specific area of interest. This is seen as a sign of commitment and intelligence! Maybe if we fostered known interests at school during the earlier days of our education many of us would feel more valued and there might be less school refusal and less loss of motivation?

Can inclusion work?

I believe that inclusion means finding ways to work with difference. When such efforts are made, yes, inclusion can work for many individuals. This is so especially when the school, area of employment and society at large are committed to making it work, and where they are willing to listen to the needs of the individual and their families. However, it should not be assumed that inclusion, on all levels, means the same thing for everyone.

For those of us who are AS individuals, inclusion will mean several things: providing a sensory environment that considers our sensory needs (they vary from individual to individual); adapting educational curricula and timetables to accommodate our differing learning styles; providing a classroom and work environment that is calm and structured, and that uses natural lighting as far as possible (no fluorescent lights that are a trigger for epilepsy); and making arrangements for lots of one-to-one support rather than a permanent group focus.

The difficulty is that very few schools, departments and places of work or leisure are equipped to meet these needs, either with respect to building layout and equipment, or with the necessary staff teaching. Therefore, inclusion sometimes increases the sense of isolation and despair, rather than fostering a sense of belonging.

Special schools and sheltered 'workshops'

Perhaps our thinking about special schools and sheltered employment options are coloured by prejudice? We tend to think of them in terms of intellectual disability or 'special needs' and even of 'second class' or lower standards. Maybe this could be changed by how we market a particular programme? When I was growing up, if you were clever you went to grammar school, the 'special school for clever kids'. If you did not do so well, you went to a secondary school. There have always been 'grades' in our thinking. You might be a 'straight A' student or you might be good with English or art... It seems to be human nature to place people into categories.

Inclusion and integration have similar overtones, but in reality, if we don't recognize that we are all different and that difference can be a good thing, then in defining inclusion we only foster exclusion. Placing every child into a school governed by inclusive policy but not inclusive practicalities is like trying to fit all shapes into one (or round pegs into square holes). It will not work.

Designing specific schools for particular needs may not be a bad idea. I think it could be especially good if, rather than keeping these separate from other schools, we mixed and matched as far as possible. At school, when I was with particular teachers who adapted school life for me, who bent the rules and who made me feel valuable, I did okay. 'If Wendy finds it difficult to be in class with those lights on, we will switch off the lights…' Some teachers brought in lamps from home and all the children seemed to benefit from this show of 'care'. At times, however, my difficulties were just too overwhelming and I couldn't partake in school life. I know some children whose difficulties require full-time care and assistance. They need specialized support and equipment that just isn't within the typical school budget. We should provide either a specialized unit that is equipped for their needs, or a specialized school. We need to be listening to their needs.

Labels

I am glad I have a label. My label helps me to understand who I am and why I function as I do. If we removed all the labels from canned foods how would we know what was inside the can? Rather than view labelling as separating, we can view it as informing. Why do we have such a problem with defining ability? My autism means that I am differently abled! I'm pleased we are not all the same and that I can contribute in a way that someone else might not. Teamwork is about incorporating all of our strengths, as and when they are needed. Just as at work we need our roles defined, our job descriptions and our 'parts' explained, so it is with education.

Accommodating all children with all of their needs under one roof would be marvellous. However, in my experience and that of my son, I have found it rarely works in any practical sense. Instead we have been made to feel our difference as a bad thing – a 'thing' that hangs on to us like dags on a sheep's tail. I need an environment that welcomes and celebrates who I am, not one that compares and contrasts me to others, and concludes 'you just don't fit'.

Being human and autistic means we have heaps of good things to contribute to society. We may not show our best in certain environments, just as the beat of a drum might silence the soft notes of a double bass. But, in their own right, both the drum and the double bass contribute to the musical effect. I long for an inclusive society that recognizes and welcomes difference. It might be that being part of an inclusive society means promoting the right to specific and particular environments and education for some individuals.

Bridging the gap

It is normal for some of us to feel 'disconnected' or 'separated' from social interaction as a whole. During times of one-to-one conversation, especially based around topics of our own interest, many individuals feel very much at home. They might have a sense of control and a sense of self. However, when it comes to interaction within a group, the pace and style of interaction is more difficult, and they might then choose to avoid the situation altogether. Because some people are good at leadership roles or roles where they have a clear script to operate from, they can enjoy group activity; for them, work or school might be places for building ongoing healthy social interaction.

I think that this is so for many of us, because in non-defined group activity it's too difficult to work out what is supposed to happen. Even in situations that are considered normal for typical individuals, such as maintaining friendships, our difficulties can be misinterpreted. It might appear that we are 'too intense' and people often feel uncomfortable with certain behaviours that they might not view as normal. However, these behaviours might be usual or normal for certain typical individuals and many AS individuals too, so whose normality is normal? Perhaps they both are and we need to work on acceptance of each other's differences. Technology could well be part of the answer that bridges the gaps between us.

The following extract is from Murray and Lawson (2007):

> Baroness Warnock rightly observes, '...if educated in mainstream schools, many [autistic] children are not included at all. They suffer all the pains of the permanent outsider. No political ideology should impose this on them.' Like anyone else, autistic children need to feel they belong (see Leary and Baumeister's 2000 review of research into the universal 'need to belong'). But these children tend not to get the point of the social realm in the same way as typically developing children. By the time they have cottoned on to it, if they do, they are likely already to be identified by other children as not belonging, and are at risk of becoming outcasts who are treated with scorn or hostility.
>
> What constitutes the common interest varies from moment to moment and culture to culture; but the force of the obligation to contribute is constant within every community of interest, however transient (Murray 1986). We suggest that opportunities to contribute to common interests are key to acquiring the sense of belonging that is at the heart of inclusion (which we have seen is a universal human need: Leary and Baumeister 2000).
>
> Traditionally, schools have had libraries full of books (this is what 'library' means after all!). But a new model of library has been emerging in the 21st century (exemplified in Tower Hamlets' 'Idea Stores': see www.ideastore.co.uk), in which books are just part of the scene. Such a library can have big windows, maximum daylight, no fluorescent lighting, and pay attention to reducing noise and maximizing sound absorption. It has banks of computers and printers and laminators, as well as access to the Internet. There is a soft zone with indestructible books; there is a café; and there are quiet rooms of various sizes off the main space. There are electronic whiteboards in every room, so that work on the computer can easily be shared. There are digital cameras, keyboards and audio-recorders, with software to edit the results. There is adaptive technology to suit every need, as well as computer games to share. (p.103)

In any given society it seems it is normal to share and relate within a community of common interest. For many of us as autistic individuals, the problem has been in not knowing how to do this with typical others. Once we have this sorted, though, I reckon sharing of common goals is not so problematic.

Respite for all

I was recently at a motorway service centre where one could stop for a break from the demands of driving. The services offered included bathrooms, restaurants, automatic banking facilities and hotel accommodation. One of the billboard notices captured my attention. It read: 'RestBite here!' Respite, or time away from demand, is one of those 'norms' we all need to take advantage of!

Typical families expend a large amount of energy in their efforts to understand their autistic children. For some families, therefore, respite and time out is crucial if they are to remain sane. However, respite situations are often facilitated by typical individuals who may not realize the autistic way of knowing and doing things. So, respite opportunities may only add to problems rather than relieve them!

Respite is offered to families so that both the child and the family can have some time away from the usual demands of everyday life. In order for respite to be a positive and useful experience for each family, the caregivers and the child need to rest in the knowledge that they will be understood and their needs will be accommodated. However, for these two things to happen for families living with AS, autism must be understood too.

AS is unlike any other diff-ability. Maybe this is why stress levels for families are higher than in any other disability population (Sharpley, Bitsika and Efremidis 1997). It is also very difficult for respite carers of AS individuals to appreciate some of the difficulties families experience. Making respite a positive encounter for AS individuals will depend upon appreciating how AS and TS individuals differ from one another. For this to happen effectively, respite carers need a working knowledge of AS and of the particular AS individual in their care. It is tempting to think that, if you have worked with one AS individual, you will understand all others. However, individuals with AS are more different than they are alike! Each AS individual will need structure, familiarity and a method for coping with change.

Preparation for attendance at respite care is important if the transition from home to respite is to be successful. Being introduced to the carers, the facility, the timetable and to the idea in general must be done slowly and over time. Using photographs and accompanied visits, to allow familiarity to be developed before the official respite occasion, are ideal.

After respite has commenced, any changes that might occur, where possible, need to be facilitated and explained. These can be done via pictures, story, scripts and role-play. Sudden change is terrifying for AS individuals. During the respite experience, allowing phone contact with family or a friend might be useful. For AS individuals being able to check in and access reassurance may prevent a meltdown. Allowing AS individuals to have space away from others and from group activity will assist in preventing overload. Having the 'house rules' visually displayed, and helping AS individuals to know what to expect from whom, where and how often, is also useful in preventing agitation, fear and overload. Mutual respect and acceptance of difference is part of all human development. Creating positive experiences for AS individuals and their families could mean that building trust and good communication between all concerned is more likely.

The following extracts were written several years ago when I was struggling to come to terms with my autism. If, as individuals, we were at home with who we were and felt comfortable and confident, the way I felt then might have been quite different.

> **The worst thing about *not* being considered normal**
> I feel 'disconnected' or 'separated' from social interaction as a whole. I'm extra conscious of blundering my way around any social event and try hard to keep social interaction to a minimum. The whole exercise is extremely tiring and I'm exhausted afterwards.
>
> During times of one-to-one conversation, especially based around topics of my own interest, I feel really good. I have a sense of control and a sense of self. However, when it comes to interaction with a group, I tend to avoid the situation, unless I am leading it in some way.

I think that I do this because it's too difficult to work out what is supposed to happen. I have also noticed that maintaining friendships seems to be quite difficult – I have been told that I am 'too intense'. I would really like to be taken seriously and have 'normal friends'. I do have a couple, but...it is difficult to have a friend.

The *best* thing about being autistic is:
The quiet and peaceful feeling of my own space which enables me to focus upon a desired object, e.g. a coloured sign, butterfly, bird, etc.

It's like having blinkers on. I can stay focused for hours. This has meant that being committed to the study area of my choice has been great. Whilst other students have become tired, bored, distracted and pressured, I am in my element. The only drawback to this is that I can only study in a quiet place. Any background noise, such as radio, TV, people, etc. appear to take away my ability to think. So, when people are talking and I need to think I have to tell them to be quiet. Other people tell me I'm not normal, and say they find it difficult to share things with me that they feel and think. I often wonder why we can't have both. Surely we need times to think, times to talk and times just to be?

In conclusion of this chapter I know that the journey to discovery of who one is can be long and tedious. Ultimately, however, self-acceptance needs to precede acceptance of other. However difficult the journey towards understanding and accepting of self is, it's a journey we all need to take. The view from the top of the hill is worth it!

CHAPTER 9

The Mismeasure of Autism

The Basis for Current Autism 'Advocacy'

By Estée Klar-Wolfond

Introduction

We take for granted that women have the same rights as men. We have come to acknowledge that women can still be women in the workplace and not a male simulacrum. Women can be both different *and* equal.

A man named Protagoras (c.485–410BC) may have laid the grounds for many struggles for equality when he said: 'Man is the measure of all things.' Against this exemplar, a woman can never measure up. If equality means to be exactly like one other than yourself, there is no equality. For example, if a woman attempts to be like a man, a woman's true equality can never be achieved. In her book *The Mismeasure of Woman* Carol Tavris encapsulates the legal dilemma of sexual equality when she says:

> As in medicine, the law regards the male as the legal standard of a human being. Therefore, women may be treated like men, in which case they are equal to them, or not like men, in which case they are deficient or special. But they are never treated specifically as women. There is no concept in the law of what is normal for women. (Tavris 1992, p.106)

Similarly, we have no concept in our current jurisprudence, or our medicine, of what is normal for an autistic person. When we seek to educate and improve the quality of life for persons with disabilities such as autism, is this not the right question: *What kinds of help do autistics need in order to contribute to society as autistic people?*

According to Davis (1997) the French statistician Adolph Quetelet (1796–1847)

> contributed the most to a generalized notion of the normal as an imperative. He noticed that the 'law of error', used by astronomers to locate a star by plotting all the sightings and then averaging the errors, could be equally applied to the distribution of human features such as height and weight. He took it a further step of formulating the concept of 'l'homme moyen' or the average man. Quetelet maintained that this *abstract human* was the average of all human attributes in a given country. For the average man, Quetelet wrote in 1835: '*all things will occur in conformity* with the mean results obtained for a society'. (p.11; emphasis added)

Quetelet, a founder of statistics, may have laid the groundwork for larger intentions. What happens to those in our society who do not conform to abstract measures? Is there only one kind of normal? Of course, when we measure every type of human being against these statistical 'norms', many people will inevitably fall into the margins. The danger is, when we truly believe that there is only one kind of normal, others begin to be devalued and become subject to submission. Christine Littleton, Professor of Law at UCLA, says: 'Efforts to achieve equality through precisely equal treatment, therefore, are doomed to fail, because men and women are not starting from the same place' (cited in Tavris 1992, p.107).

So, too, autistic people are not starting from the same place as the majority. Instead, our view of autistic individuals was recently exemplified in Jenny McCarthy's characterization of her son's autistic behaviours as 'boo boos' on *The View* and on *Larry King Live* – an affectionate way of calling autistic behaviour *wrong*.

What do her characterizations of her child mean to those people who are autistic or have other disabilities? Do we value people only when they have overcome their disability or, as we now hear, 'have recovered'? It seems Jenny is unaware of what autistic people have to say about what it really means to be disabled.

My thesis is that the struggle of autistic people, like what happened to women, is the result of this 'mismeasurement' against subjective norms. The way we market autism – from advocacy and education through to therapies and treatments – stems from this mismeasure. Neither valued for their neurological difference, nor heard regarding their perspectives on the social implications of their disability, autistic people have been subject to treatment that seeks to normalize them or, as history has shown, institutionalize and segregate them. Given IQ tests and other measures constructed for the typical majority and not originally intended for them (see Gould 1996), autistic people come to be considered 'wrong', 'abnormal', 'sick', 'victims' and 'hopeless', and are therefore continually set up for failure.

Biology and culture are always entwined with experience, and these experiences are variable for every individual – not determined. That said, autism is not an aberrance, but a challenge *and* a way to live and experience the world. This is not 'wrong', but atypical, unique, and referred to as a 'way of being'. In other words, autistic people are 'normal' in their own right. Paul Collins, a father of an autistic child, wrote in his book:

> Autists are described by others – and by themselves – as aliens among humans. But there's an irony to this for precisely the opposite is true. They are us, and to understand them is to begin to understand what it means to be human. Think of it: a disability is usually defined in terms of what is missing. A child tugs at his or her parents and whispers, 'Where's that man's arm?' But autism is an ability and a disability: it as much about what is abundant as what is missing, an over expression of the very traits that make our species unique. Other animals are social, but only humans are capable of abstract logic. The autistic outhuman the humans and we can scarcely recognize the result. (Collins 2004, p.161)

Their common experiences and characteristics unite autistic people as a community in which they can talk about the social prejudices against them. Therefore, it is necessary and important to discuss what is 'normal' for autistic people before we can begin to discuss ways in which to raise both awareness and support.

Misguided advocacy

> *The people can always be brought to the bidding of the leaders. That is easy. All you have to do is tell them they are being attacked and denounce the pacifists for lack of patriotism and exposing the country to danger. It works the same in any country. (Hermann Goering,* The Nuremburg Diary*)*

Fear is embedded in the names of some our most visible autism organizations. Names like Generation Rescue, Cure Autism Now, Fighting Autism.org and Safe Minds make us all question – just whose mind is considered to be *safe*?

Leaders in autism are called advocates. They are running schools, they are scientists (considered experts) and the heads of autism organizations, like Autism Speaks, the largest autism charity in the US. Last I looked, this charity had a total annual budget of 60 million dollars, mostly dedicated to, as Hillary Clinton so clearly stated in a campaign speech for President, 'preventing and curing *anything* along the autism spectrum' (a clip from the speech was published on YouTube – see www.youtube.com/watch?v=8wØx3vkkyKs).

We hear from our own Canadian applied behaviour analysis (ABA) advocates that 'autism is a living nightmare', a 'prison that locks the child within', and recently in a newspaper article in which Michelle Dawson and I were interviewed in all but too few paragraphs for the other side of the autism story, ABA advocates were still insisting that 'autism is like a death in the family', and it's all 'doom' (Collier 2007). (I say 'still' because after years of requests from autistic people and parents regarding the inappropriate use of alarmist and misleading language in order to garner political support, this community still insists on using it.)

Of course, doom is the path to nowhere – it leads to an overall perception that, with autism, we live in a dark tunnel that we cannot escape. It leads us to desperation. With that model, there is only one hope – to cure autism as quickly as possible.

In Autism Speak's *Autism Everyday* video, which was acclaimed at the Sundance Film Festival, Allison Tepper Singer, Senior Vice President of Autism Speaks, talks about wanting to drive off the George Washington Bridge with her autistic daughter – while her daughter is in the same room. While many of us can relate to the frustration she feels in not finding an appropriate school, many autistic people and parents were shocked that she said this on a national fundraising film; moreover, with perhaps a belief that her daughter wouldn't understand her, which is all too typical of how autistic people are referred to – 'not aware', or 'like they're not even in the room'. The consequences of such beliefs are evident in the example of Ashley X ('The Pillow Angel'). Ashley, diagnosed with profound multiple impairments, was only nine years old when she began growth attenuation therapy. At the instigation of her parents she was given high doses of oestrogen to bring about permanent restriction to her size and development. Ashley also underwent a hysterectomy and the removal of both her breast buds allegedly to improve her quality of life and so that she could remain under the care of her parents at home; her parents claim that by controlling her size they are able to continue lifting her.

Undoubtedly, the so-called 'treatment' has raised significant questions on the legal protections and rights for the disabled, society's assumptions about what disability means in terms of cognition and sentience, limitations on the family over proposed treatments for their child, the subjectivity of definitions of *quality of life* entwined in overall assumptions about disability, society's prejudice towards disabled individuals, and the issues surrounding the meaning of suffering against the medicalization of disabilities.

Singer says that the only reason she didn't drive off the bridge is that she had another daughter at home (who, by the way, is not autistic). Her non-autistic daughter goes on to say that she wished she didn't have an autistic sister and that she didn't want anyone to see her, which eerily takes us back to the last century, where parents were made to feel ashamed for having disabled children and so sent them to institutions. The video makes autism appear horrible and challenging beyond imagination. Autism is portrayed as dark, driving parents to want to commit murder – and sadly, some do (Smith 2007).

Living in the land of 'what-ifs' is not a denial. It's a necessary step in creating new paradigms that are more appropriate for the realities that both autistic people and parents face. Autism Speaks has a major problem: they are raising money for a group of people who do not necessarily want to be cured and to whom they don't listen. Autistic people face a problem: they are the constant subjects of disrespect, hatred and dangerous treatments, and are at risk of annihilation. Parents are at risk: they don't know what to do and where to turn, so that they risk harming themselves and their autistic children.

Based on the different but equal premise of autistic individuals in our society, and assuming that many parents are frustrated with the lack of schools and understanding, what if:

- we didn't have to see dark videos (or hear the messages) like this, but were congratulated at the time of diagnosis? (seems like a jump, but just imagine)
- a doctor smiled (instead of frowned) and explained that many autistic people already contribute to society – they are musicians, scientists, computer programmers, poets and writers, and there are other autistic people who are contributing in different yet valuable ways?
- doctors helped parents see that autism is a part of the human condition?
- parents were educated and supported about the challenges autistic people face in addition to the abilities (so we can see that all children will have challenges, get sick, bring us joys, and that the outcome of any child is not fixed or predetermined)?
- parents had access to good schools where our children are accepted and included, and autistic skills were honoured and built upon?
- parents were not made to feel isolated or have to answer questions every day about why their children are different, or subject to advice on how to fix their children?
- children (the non-verbal ones) were taught to use a communication device, so they could say 'I love you, Mommy [or Daddy]', and we learned how to value behavioural communication?

What if our autism organizations fought for this? I am sure that others can tweak or expand the list I've provided.

Potentially lethal is this combination of two dissociated concepts: *acceptance* and *cure*. Canadian autism societies are claiming that they have to be 'non-partisan', and so they support nearly everything despite a lack of empirical evidence, like biomedical intervention, applied behavioural and other therapies – and they do so while advocating acceptance. In a month-long investigation, the Kennedy Krieger Institute found over 180 treatments and therapies being promoted, which they said 'almost all require a checkbook and/or credit card' (Interactive Autism Network 2007). How many times have we heard well-intentioned parents say things like *we have to try anything and everything*? Our autism societies are not properly filtering the information in order to protect autistic people. Instead of supporting the people they claim to work on behalf of, our societies are still advocating for the cure and remediation of autistic people. They do so by suggesting that some of these 'therapies' work by tacitly endorsing unproven treatments on their websites. As they are considered authorities to which people turn, we must hold them accountable.

This pressure has to come principally from parents. Autistic people will not be fully taken notice of as long as autism continues to be viewed as a tragedy that we must try anything to cure. When autistic people are sometimes allowed a voice within charities, this can appear to be merely appeasement in the face of an autistic civil rights movement, rather than a genuine move towards listening to the autistic voice.

Helping people manage a disability, however, is not akin to saying that they must become normal. While acceptance doesn't mean acquiescence, it is difficult to tie it in with 'recovery'. If autistic people are normal in their own right, then there is no need for recovery; there is only need for support.

What if our organizational leaders followed the similar example of Krista Flint of the Canadian Down Syndrome Society and said *I can't imagine the world without an autistic person in it.* (Krista Flint said 'I cannot imagine a world without a person with Down syndrome in it' in response to a newspaper article on doctors recommending more prenatal testing to prevent Down syndrome births.) What if our autism organizations renamed themselves perhaps like this:

- Generation Rescue could become Generation Respect
- Safe Minds could become Unique Minds
- Cure Autism Now could become Celebrate Autism Now
- The Autism Autoimmunity Project could become The Autism Acceptance Project.

If we renamed our organizations, what might the public, parents and scientists think and feel about autism and how might it guide our actions and attitudes towards autistic individuals?

Misfired intentions

We all know the saying 'The road to hell was paved with good intentions', or as Robert Herrick said, 'Hell is paved with good Samaritans.' In response to my criticisms of Jenny McCarthy, who characterized her son's autistic behaviours as 'boo boos', people say, 'Well at least she's raising awareness.' But is this the right kind of awareness? Does the marketing model for, say, curing cancer fit the needs of autistic people in terms of their human rights and the accommodations and supports they need in order to contribute to society as they are?

Nietzsche didn't think highly of benevolence, seeing it as an act in order to keep the benevolent person in a superior position. He said:

> ...we should make a distinction in benevolence between the impulse to appropriate and the impulse to submit, and ask whether it is the stronger or the weaker that feels benevolent. Joy and desire appear together in the stronger that wants to transform something into a function; joy and the wish to be desired appear together in the weaker that wants to become a function. Pity is essentially of the former type; an agreeable impulse of the instinct for appropriation at the sight of what is weaker. But it should be kept in mind that 'strong' and 'weak' are relative concepts. (Nietzsche 1974, p.176)

To pity others is to put oneself into a superior position. It oppresses others, which is why autistic people often identify with other social movements like the gay rights movement or the black civil rights movement in North America (Savarese 2007).

Prejudice is best described as applying a different set of standards to one set of people over another. We have to consider that we would not like to be referred to in the way that charities have begun to encapsulate autistic existence through the puzzle image. The puzzle piece is a suggestion that autistic people are the mystery, again putting the burden on them to metamorphose into something that *we* can understand. Instead of looking at ourselves and our own bias and working harder to accept autistic individuals, we are gung-ho on curing them to make ourselves feel good, and relieve our burden.

We also have to ask the important question of why we seek to ameliorate autism or 'recover' it. Are we seeking to obtain the 'normal' child we thought we were supposed to have? Are we in search of the elusive 'perfection'? Or do we *accept* the child we do have? Do we *celebrate* that child, while trying to help them manage some of the more challenging aspects of their disability? Do we assist autistics to be the best they can be because we *understand and value* autistic people? Perhaps the answer is in not throwing the baby out with the bathwater, but rather, in 'merging help with respect' (Kunc and Van Der Klift 1994).

Many autistic people have rallied against the puzzle image by stating 'I am not a puzzle, I am a person', and have petitioned against Autism Speaks in their campaign Autism Speaks: Don't Speak for Me. Yet the public never hears about this. Autistic people are still kept on the margins.

By examining the way autism is represented by our celebrities, charities, therapists and some of our scientists, we can illustrate that bias and prejudice are not limited to race or religion, but also to people with disabilities; and it is the most tolerated form of prejudice today. We live in a society that glorifies celebrities who in turn support causes about which many of them understand little. When philanthropy is the 'new black', we do not reflect enough on the consequences of what we support. In short, it is probably worthy of our consideration when the disabled community says en masse: 'We do not need another Jerry Lewis.' (The US comedian and actor Jerry

Lewis courted controversy in the 1990s with remarks about people with muscular dystrophy being like 'half a person'.)

What if we changed the marketing model so that instead of eliciting pity, we focused on gathering respect?

To construct a new marketing model for autism charities, what if:

- we let autistic people speak and ensure that there are more autistic people running our autism society boards and that there are at least an equal number of autistic people at all our conferences as there are non-autistic ones?
- we regard their lives with honour and respect?
- we listen to their experiences in order to learn and become sensitive to their needs?
- we approach carefully and learn from autistics on how to educate and support them instead of imposing what we think they need and how we think they should be taught?
- we believed that they are truly different *and* equal?

Misrepresenting recovery

As advocates and celebrities continue to spotlight autistic deficiencies in the name of better 'treatments', and refer to autistic people as 'hopeless' without recovery, they not only acrimoniously exclude autistics from the dialogue, they are tacitly suggesting they are alien from the human race. Autistics who ask for accommodation are insulted and ignored, even hated. Parents on the Evidence of Harm discussion list, named after David Kirby's book which blames vaccines for causing autism, and parents who advocate for ABA as the *only* treatment to cure autism, have demonstrated their view of autistic individuals, whom they have described as:

- hopeless
- doomed without ABA
- inappropriate
- disruptive
- weird

- government mercury vaccine poisoned kids
- a parent's worst nightmare syndrome
- equal opportunity disasters
- walking biohazards.

Unfortunately, the list of pejorative references is much longer than I've written here. Further, while some would argue that 'inappropriate, disruptive and weird' are not in and of themselves, 'pejorative', they are bully-words. Instead, we must view unusual people as a natural part of a whole range of humanity. To see more of these references from the biomedical advocates, read Kathleen Seidel's open letter to David Kirby (Seidel 2005). It is also worthwhile to add here that many autistics who have spoken out against pejorative referencing and dangerous treatments have been stalked, been the recipients of hate mail, and name-called on websites expressing their anger and dislike of autism and autistic people.

Autistic adults who speak out against autism charities and interventionists are called 'not autistic' by those parents who wish to paint a dark picture of autism for funding purposes, because if autistic people can communicate, they do damage to the marketing model. G.K. Chesterson said: 'Art is limitation; the essence of every picture is the frame.' Autistics don't fit into their frame. They do not conform to the pity paradigm. They are not hopeless enough.

Society cannot recognize, within this overwhelming autism-is-a-fate-worse-than-death framework, the innate value of the autistic person, and we do not understand the challenges of their, in many cases, 'invisible disability'. People have a difficulty in understanding that there is no normal or abnormal in autism. There is only dissonance. There is, as Paul Collins (2004) said, ability and disability. With every disability, everyone is valuable and has potential. Society cannot wrap its collective head around the fact that some people are different *and* will require more support and accommodation throughout their lifetime in order to contribute. We tend to overrate independence and normalcy as worthy goals, whilst forgetting that we are all, in fact, interdependent. We do seem, however, to understand quite well the notion of handicap in golf. The

United States Golf Association website says: 'Since its inception USGA Handicap System has made it possible for golfers of differing abilities to enjoy fair competition.'

We use a handicap to equalize the playing field by identifying what one's handicap is and then accommodating that in the game. Yet in autism, if I may borrow the words of Stephen Gould, we 'parse complex and continuous reality into divisions of two' (Gould 1996, p.27). We base everything on our need for proof of either competence or incompetence, and if you are considered incompetent you cannot participate in a fair game. Yet what about making room for both – accommodating the handicap in order to make room for the possibilities?

Consider this anonymous quote from an autistic person on the Autistics.org website, discussing the accommodation and greater understanding of autism, and the current lack thereof:

> They see you talking; therefore, talking must be easy. They see you moving around; therefore, motion must be effortless... Maybe it's like being a duck – you appear to be gliding smoothly across the water surface, but underneath the water where people can't see, you're busy paddling like hell...
>
> ...I finally got independent study 'privileges' at the end of the year, after my parents, of all people, started pushing for it, but everyone was very adamant on the point that 'in the future, you won't get this. You'll have to do it the same way as everyone else, with everyone else.'
>
> I don't think people get it. I expect nothing. I expect nothing to be given to me. I expect to be called a liar and manipulator and an excuse-maker and to be told that the system owes me nothing and that I can sink or swim. I expect to be forced to plead, beg and grovel in order to get any kind of accommodations at school, extended deadlines and the like, and to be seen as a manipulative liar if I still can't do it.

We require an urgent shift of perception to view autistics as atypical, as opposed to 'wrong', and autism as a different and *valuable* way of being. Autistic people, much like women, have the right to be, therefore, different *and* equal and worthy of accommodation. They do not have to change themselves into normal-seeming simulacrums. This is not a worthy goal in assisting autistic individuals.

In the wake of celebrities speaking as experts on autism, let's step back a bit and consider *again* that autistic people are missing from our public dialogue – they are not seen on *Larry King Live*, *Oprah* or *The View*, for example. Although Amanda Baggs' blog Ballastexistenz and her video from YouTube 'In My Language' were featured on CNN in 2007. In no other charity for any other disease or disability do we view such an obvious absence of the people autism charities represent. We get to see autistic people only in extremes in the media – once in a while as tag-alongs of parental lost-dreams, or as models of recovery – all usually representing a charity or special biomedical treatment group. We rarely get to hear what autistic people really think about what's going on or what's happening to them in their lives.

Yet, there are a multitude of organizations and autistic self-advocates (and the list is thankfully growing) out there. I know that as a mother, I've learned a lot from them. But I wonder how many of you have heard of them?

Organizations that speak for autistic people

- Abnormal Diversity
- Action for Autism
- Along The Spectrum
- Asperger's Association of New England
- Aspies for Freedom
- Autcom
- Autism Diva
- Autism Network International
- Autistic Adults Picture Project
- Autistic Advocacy
- Autistic Self-Advocacy Network
- Autistics.org
- GRASP
- No Autistics Allowed
- Oddizm
- PosAutive
- Pre Rainman Autism
- Whose Planet Is It Anyway?

Autism self-advocates

- Alex Bain
- Amanda Baggs
- Larry Bissonnette
- Laura Tisoncik

Anne Carpenter
Ari Newman
Barbara Moran
Bartholomew Cubbins
Brian Henson
David Goodman
Frank Klein
Jamie Burke
Jane Meyerding
Jenn Seybert
Jim Sinclair
Joel Smith
John Gelmon
Kassiane Sibley
Kathy Grant
Larry Arnold
Liane Holliday Willey
Lucy Blackman
Martine Stonehouse
Matthew Schuster
Michael Moon
Michelle Dawson
Mike Hoover
Patty Clark
Phil Schwarz
Ralph Smith
Robert W. Cutler
Sandra Radisch
Sharisa Joy Kochmeister
Stephen Shore
Sue Rubin
Vernon Smith

I have limited space here, but there are many more individuals and self-advocates than I've listed.

We must seek their input! Yet, without consulting them or considering the social implications just described, Canadian comic actor Eugene Levy will rally behind ABA/IBI as the only treatment or therapy to remediate autism, while Jenny McCarthy has already begun her cries for curing autism through biomedical intervention and diet. She is the new spokesperson for TACA – Talk About Curing Autism Now.

What kind of authority do celebrities bring to autism, when, as Jenny McCarthy also admitted on *Larry King Live*, she has never once met an autistic adult? Eugene Levy reportedly only met his young autistic cousin the day before the press announcement that he was going to represent Canadian ABA advocates (Mick 2007), and Bill Cosby, referring to an autistic child, bumbled, 'It's…it's like he's not even in the room.' These are all non-autistic people who seem to be missing the point because they are not engaging with a myriad of autistic people.

Celebrity endorsements, however, are powerful motivators – from getting you to buy jewellery on The Shopping Network, to giving your money for AIDS research – celebrities can bring in the big bucks, not to mention a great deal of awareness and attention to a product or a cause. That said, autism awareness has a dark side.

Autism is not cancer or AIDS. Those diseases are life-threatening, while autism is life-long. There is a real difference between marketing for cancer, AIDS, saving Darfur, and the marketing for an autism 'cure'. As a former marketer for health charities, I am more than aware of the temptation and effectiveness of using the word 'cure' for raising money. I was the developer for the first Click for the Cure Campaign for the Arthritis Society. When charities only answer the call of non-autistic parents as the people who are 'suffering' – we can say this because it is only their voices we hear – we have not an organization for autistic people, but one for parents who cannot resist the siren call of a normal child, or are in fear that if they do not try anything, they are bad parents.

Further, as I have already noted, autism is a disability, not a disease. Yet, some neurologists and other advocates still want to portray autism as a 'whole body medical condition', despite the lack of evidence to support that notion. Consider, also, that we are diagnosing anything and everything that comprises the human condition, rather than evaluating the circumstances around autistic experience – the good and the painful – and asking what that means and feels like. We can and are pathologizing human experience, and we do so by adding in our bias – our mismeasures. We should not misread the disability as a medical condition, but take a look at how we can assist the disability while dealing with some medical aspects that can result in any human being.

Carol Tavris notes that we have done the same with women's natural biology and cultural experience. She says:

> Everywhere we look today, we see that the normal changes of menstruation and menopause are increasingly being regarded as diseases, problems and causes of women's emotional woes and

> practical difficulties. In particular, biomedical researchers have taken a set of bodily changes and packaged them into 'Premenstrual Syndrome', and sold them back to women as a disorder, a problem that needs treatment and attention. (Tavris 1992, p.133)

She notes that doctors have listed over 150 symptoms associated with PMS – many of which would apply to men! For these millions of sick women, myself included, there are a myriad of products we can buy – prescription medications, over-the-counter remedies, herbs, diets – and many medical support groups. And the same could be said of the autism industry that uses fear in its sales pitches.

'A physician writing in the *Wall Street Journal* estimated that the illness of PMS costs US industry 8% of its total wage bill' (Tavris 1992, Introduction). Similarly, we hear that autistics cost the Canadian economy $4.6 billion (Autsim Society Canada 2004, p.10) – so ominous is the number that it hangs like a bounty over the heads of autistic individuals. Incidentally, I haven't seen any comparable numbers showing how much autistics contribute and add to the Canadian economy. But nothing can compete with the 'financial burden of autistic people' or a 'cost to industry' framework to sell a method, a product or a cure. It's the strongest marketing tactic around.

Let's compare. According to Tavris (1992), the media has reported PMS as:

- 'The Monthly Menace' – *Science News*
- 'The Internal Earthquake' – *The Orange County Register*
- 'In a tea factory in China, almost 80% of women suffered from PMS' – *Psychology Today*
- 'Premenstrual syndrome remains as baffling to researchers as it is troublesome to women' – *Psychology Today.*

Autism has been marketed and promoted with such phrases as:

- 'a mysterious upsurge' – *The New York Times*
- 'a baffling outbreak' – *CBS News*
- 'cases are exploding in number' – *TIME*
- 'and no one knows why' – *USA Today.*

There are frequent references to an autism epidemic. Yet as Gernsbacher, Dawson and Goldsmith (2005) deduce, 'Epidemics solicit causes; false epidemics solicit false causes' (see also Grinker 2007). In order to understand this, let's take a look briefly at epidemiology, the study into the causes of epidemics.

Epidemiology, says Gary Taubes in a *New York Times Magazine* article, 'is the here-today, gone-tomorrow nature of medical wisdom. There are, after all, an infinite number of wrong hypotheses for every right one, so the odds are always against any particular hypothesis being true' (Taubes 2007).

The media will publish a press release on any study, not yet proven, on autism. It might behove us to remember a journalist's maxim: 'Yesterday's paper wraps today's garbage.' Most of what we hear is speculation, not yet fact. Still, we sell products and build health policy on what the media reports. Little research is undertaken by many of our journalists into the real sides of the autism 'story', regardless of the Society of Professional Journalists Code of Ethics which states under the heading 'Seek Truth and Report It': 'Tell the story of diversity and magnitude of the human experience boldly' and 'Avoid stereotyping by race, geography, sexual orientation, disability, physical appearance or social status.' Sensation and doom sells, and many reporters have become lazy. We have to be sceptical about what the media reports because, as Taubes (2007) says: 'After all, it's the first claim in any scientific endeavour that is most likely to be wrong.'

We must also remember that there are, and have been, real life-threatening epidemics out there. Polio and AIDS are but two examples, and our scientists cannot conclude that we have an autism epidemic, but it sure is a scary word. Roy Grinker said:

> Epidemic is a powerful concept. It implies danger and incites fear, calling up associations with plagues that can sweep through the streets, something contagious in the air you breathe or in the food you eat, threatening the one's you love. With autism the label 'epidemic' sounds both frightening and tragic. (Grinker 2007, p.5)

Those who profit from the cultivation of despair broadcast catastrophic depictions, and the true meaning of epidemic has come to have little meaning. Yet, 'epidemic' is a powerful reality. The loose use of the term cheapens it and minimizes the significance of true epidemics.

Though we know that autism is not a disease, claimants, like Jenny McCarthy and TACA, are proselytizing and marketing diets, supplements and therapies and suggest that, with them, autism can now be 'recovered' – a rather tricky semantics exercise in stating that autistic people can't be cured but they can be 'healed', but not in all cases, and oh, they will likely still have 'boo boos'. All said, because they are already 'damaged' and 'broken' ('Broken' is how Dr Kartzinel referred to autistic people on *Larry King Live*).

In September 2007, the CBC reported that Canadian doctors warned not to give a child under the age of 12 a multivitamin. We've all received conflicting messages about what is going to make us live longer and healthier one day, to find that the next day what we thought was good for us just might make us sick. It's also the basis for a lot of latitude in the promotion of autism 'remedies' (and causes, for that matter); the same argument could be applied to vaccines. However, we have to date no evidence to prove that vaccines cause autism after rigorous scientific research.

To recover autism, autistic kids are to go to specific doctors, some under the DAN! Protocol (otherwise known as Defeat Autism Now!), and use a variety of medicines, supplements and therapies to 'heal' the child. The lists and 'protocols' are ominous:

5-HTP	Calcium	Curcumin
Acidophilus	Caprylic acid	Cysteine Sulfate
Active Charcoal	Carnosine	Detox phases 1,2,3,4
ALA	Chromium	Digestive enzymes
Amino acids	Cobiotic companion	Dimercaptosuccinic acid
Arabinogalactan	Cod liver oil	DMAE
Bifidus	Coenzyme Q-10	Essential fatty acids
Biotin	Creatine	Evening primrose oil
Fish oil	Magnesium	Quercitin

Folinic acid	Melatonin	Saccharomyces boulardii
GABA	Methionine	S-Adenosyl methionine
Gama oryzanol	Methyl-B-12	Selenium
Garlic	N-acetyl-carnitine	Silymarin
Glutathione	N-acetyl-cysteine	Taurine
Hyperbaric Oxygen Chamber	Niacin	TMG
Infrared Sauna	Olive leaf extract	Vitamin A
Inositol	Omega-3	Vitamin B-12
Iron	Oral gamma globulin	Vitamin B-6
L-Arginine	Oregano oil	Vitamin C
Lauricidin	Pantothenic acid	Vitamin D
L-Glutamine	Phosphatidylcholine	Vitamin E
L-Theanine	Probiotics	
Lysine	Pycnogenol	

The full lists would be dauntingly longer than those I've provided.

Would we subject a neurotypical child to dozens or more of supplements, detoxification therapies and 'healing' medications, without scientific evidence to support that it is safe? I doubt it. Yet, for autistic kids, taking substantial risks seems to be okay. And to make them what? – Better at maths, quicker on the sports field, or well-mannered? Is this fair?

The consequence is not only that autistic people are stigmatized as a result of gross generalizations that one thing can cause or remedy autism, but also that the lives and health of many autistic children are in danger.

Still, the volume and weight of these messages that bamboozle and intimidate a confused public – delivered by 'doctors' and celebrities – is compelling. More parents are choosing not to vaccinate their children, exposing them to the risk of life-threatening diseases. Some children, who have undergone chelation therapy in order to 'recover' from autism, have died from it (see e.g. Centers for Disease Control and Prevention 2006). Why are we risking our children's health? Does the benefit really outweigh the risk? There might be people who say, absolutely yes. There are ABA and biomedical advocates telling our politicians and public that 'autism is a fate worse than death' (see Freeman 2003). If you really believed them, you might agree that anything, even a child's life, is worth the cost.

While I do not wish to alienate families who are undergoing a struggle to accept, understand and raise their autistic child, I do believe that we can rally far more support by including autistic people. I do believe that all parents are concerned with the welfare of their children in terms of safety, rights and opportunities. I don't believe that the doom scenarios are really helping parents cope, or are assisting autistic people in living healthy and productive lives.

What kind of world do we want to live in?

So, here's the rub: If you believe that autism is 'hopeless' without recovery, when the truth is that autistic people mature and progress *while still being autistic*, then 'recovery' will be seen to have worked. To put it another way, if you believe that autism is hopeless, then autistic people are bound to recover because there's no where to go but up. You've already put them at the bottom of the pile.

But what if we are witnessing and measuring not recovery as such, but just the nature and variability of autistic development? What if, with such awareness, the circumstances surrounding that development were positive and nurturing, and valued the nature of autistic intelligence and ability, while respecting and accommodating the more disabling aspects of autism? The research by Dawson *et al.* (2007) from the University of Montreal on the nature of autistic intelligence is exciting to many of us because it is the first of its kind in autism, which takes this different and equal premise into account. It does not base autistic ability as the reverse of human pathology, and it is hoped future studies will be conducted with the autistics-as-valuable measure.

Imagine what the world would look like if:

- autism ability was valued, not greeted with arm's-length fascination, or perceived as weird genius
- autism was viewed as natural
- autism was okay
- autism was understood in terms of a different way of being, knowing, learning and behaving
- autistic behaviours were viewed as a different way of communicating rather than disruptive and problematic.

What if we could develop support for:

- anxiety and physical issues that took into account the external issues and seeking to modify the environment rather than the behaviour?
- non-autistics in sensitivity training with autistic people doing the teaching?
- socialization-understanding versus becoming a normal socializer?
- training and augmentative communication with Assistive Augmentative Communication (AAC) or Assistive Technology (AT)?
- autism education versus remediation?
- inclusion as a win–win situation for both non-disabled and disabled citizens?

What if we defined the 'mosaic' of support and education for autistic people with the premise that everyone progresses from their own starting point? Perhaps a mission for the way we educate could derive from this:

> *Teaching autistic children, as opposed to wasting their time, may be the difference between teaching them to be normal as the sole goal versus teaching them about the world and enabling them, with the appropriate tools, to communicate their feelings about it.*

I define teaching my own son by valuing his response while building bridges for him to communicate and navigate the world. I do not judge Adam by his behaviours, nor do I measure his intelligence through typical responses. His responses and behaviours are the valuable ways he communicates with me and from which we can build together.

Although some societies have positive aspects to their campaigns, most are shrouded by remedies and cures, rather than support for living good lives with autism. Such mixed messages lessen the resolve and integrity of otherwise positive campaigns. But, with the notable exceptions of the Autism Acceptance Project in Canada and other self-advocacy groups, there is nothing in our current autism advocacy or marketing campaigns that sets out explicitly to destigmatize autism, celebrate autistic existence, improve quality of life *with* autism, advocate for a mosaic of support so that all autistic people can be served, and demand the highest standard of scientific research. The dialogue today, sadly, is increasingly exclusive and polemic, and the marketing-of-despair model seems to be set in stone, while a few of us gather to advocate for basic human rights. As there are many smaller groups and individuals working toward the same goal throughout the world, we need to consolidate so that people can *see* us and the real issues autistic people, of all ages, face. So-called 'advocacy' groups that resort to bullying and exclusion must not intimidate us for our efforts.

'What if?' in research – Measure of value

We are, however, bound to the concrete need for truth when the cards are so stacked against autistic people as different *and* equal. Currently there is too much focus on research that seeks to prevent and cure many disabilities, not just autism, instead of conducting more research into the nature of human intelligence. There is not enough research into how to improve the lives of autistic people, notwithstanding the many families who feel they have benefited from having autistic and other disabled children. We need to see and hear the positive stories parents can express, and persuade our scientists to conduct the research that will benefit disabled people living in society.

Patricia E. Bauer, a journalist and a mother of a daughter with Down syndrome, said:

> ...we live in a time in history in which the faces of our loved ones have come to symbolize something in the public mind that is very much at odds with our life experience. People see our family members and think what they've been taught to think. They think our children are tragedies. Yet we who are privileged to live with them know that, despite some of the frustrations of day-to-day existence, our lives are also filled with possibility and love and joy. (Bauer 2007)

King *et al.* (2006) conducted some research with families with autism and Down syndrome, documenting the positive life changes that families have experienced with their disabled children. Such accounts and studies are important if we seek to support and empower families, and improve the quality of life for people with disabilities.

With genetics research and preventive diagnostics a thriving billion-dollar industry, we are, says Patricia Bauer, 'developing better ways of spotting and eliminating these people before they are born...doctors [have] failed to notice that they have embarked upon the elimination of an entire class of people who have a history of oppression, discrimination and exclusion' (Bauer 2007). While she is talking about Down syndrome, it really is no different for autism.

Many in our research community are already biased against autistic people – using language that dehumanizes and pathologizes them as 'abnormal' and 'mutated'. Recently, Kevin Leitch, creator of the Autism Hub, illustrated in a recent video the thoughts of Dr Jerry Kartzinel (who has 'dedicated' his practice to recovering children with autism) who said: 'Autism, as I see it, steals the soul from the child, and, if allowed, relentlessly sucks the marrow out of the family members one by one.' Dr Kartzinel himself relentlessly sucks out lifeblood with this lifeless depiction of our autistic children. We must speak out because it is precisely these kinds of words that will ostracize them and damage their self-image, not to mention their safety, if we allow it to continue.

We know that many scientists give little or no consideration to what autistic people say about their own autism, or listen to the positive stories and love we feel for our children as they are. We have an over-medicalized and, one might even say after hearing Dr Kartzinel, ruthless view of disability. Our celebrities who are 'spokespeople' for such organizations take it further and paint the doom and gloom picture of autism to a larger public that makes people fear it and want to get rid of it as quickly as possible. That's why there is no shortage of money dedicated to preventing autism. So much for protecting our most vulnerable citizens.

Scientists, says Stephen Gould, 'are good at analyzing data and critiquing conclusions of others...but rarely do they contemplate history in the sense of moral instruction' (Gould 1996, p.25). A true model of oppression, autistic people are kept at arm's length as 'patients' and 'clients', and are not welcome to participate in the overall scientific process. Autistic people are presumed to be incompetent, and therefore not considered the true 'experts' of themselves and autism. While one might argue that none of us are the true experts of our brains or DNA, we certainly have a lot to learn in the way we approach autism and autistic people.

To make our land of 'what ifs' a reality, we must insist that our scientists and clinicians, at every level, engage the input and work of our autistic citizens and exercise some self-reflection into the bias that exists within all of us, for as Darwin said: 'If the misery of our poor be caused not by the laws of nature, but by our institutions, great is our sin.'

So to just make it clear, at the time of this writing:

1. There is no scientific evidence that diets and biomedical treatments work to either 'recover' or 'cure' autism.

2. Science has tested the autism and vaccine theory, and there is no evidence to support that vaccines cause autism.

3. No credible scientists will say that there is an autism 'epidemic'.

Let us stand *with*, not speak *for*

> *Together we must rally for the accommodations, education and the supports autistics need while valuing them as autistic people. We must do so by including autistic individuals in the process and by engaging in language and with attitudes that reflect our respect for human dignity – embracing the difference and equality of all persons in our society.*

As far as celebrity endorsement goes, I support Sigourney Weaver, who recently had her photo taken alongside autistic folks at GRASP in New York (see above). The poster reads: *Not Everyone on the Autism Spectrum Wants to be Cured.*

It is an example of what our leaders and celebrities *can* do. Instead of purporting to speak for autistic people, let us, as non-autistic people, stand beside and with them. Let us become allies. As autistic self-advocate Phil Schwarz has alluded to in his writings about autistic 'allies', there is room for many more of us.

As I envision Adam as an adult, I hope there will be many more of you who will stand with him, and value him. I am so grateful to the autistic adults and youth who stand up against adversity, for it is *you* who pave the way for my son's future. He is, after all, my real star. I want him to live his life peacefully, without the constant bombardment that the sole purpose of his life is to only become like others. I watch his sweet smiling face in his new school, as he focuses on his work. I would hate for all his hard work to be funnelled into 'becoming normal'. It seems like such a waste of not only time, but of human potential.

About the author of this chapter

Estée Klar-Wolfond is the founder and executive director of The Autism Acceptance Project and a writer and public speaker. Most importantly, she is the mother of a wonderful son named Adam. This chapter was part of a keynote address at AutCom in Edmonton, 13 October 2007.

CHAPTER 10

Changing the Status Quo

There seem to be so many factors that influence an individual over the lifespan. Some theorists will argue that we are only a product of our environment; that we are born with a 'clean slate' that the world then writes upon. Other theorists suggest that we are simply a product of our genetic makeup and have no say at all in how we turn out. However, although it seems obvious that each of us is a product of genetic influences, we are also influenced by our environment and by how we have chosen (if we were free to do so) to respond to it.

Changing the status quo – so that it doesn't change me, but allows me to develop to my fullest potential – should be an available option for each of us. As we have seen in the previous chapters, typical normality is very restrictive and biased. It does not allow for difference and diversity so much as it fosters societal interests that are more concerned with making money, furthering fashion and the politics of power. In order to challenge the above and contribute to a changing, more inclusive idea of normality we each need to make a stand and take back our power. Allowing others to dictate what is normal and push our lives into oblivion has to stop. We can be part of the remedy.

Myself as a child and an adult

As an individual with autism I recognize that my experiences will, according to different sources, only represent 1 in 100 (Baird *et al.* 2006) or 1 in 58 (Baron-Cohen *et al.* 2007). Does this make them less valid? I think not, but it will mean that they are not recognized as 'the norm'. However, I'll share with you my understanding and what has moulded me to a greater extent. It is not my autism so much, but the impact of those who took a risk and saw potential in me that others missed. The biggest impact upon one's future might be how Others have impacted upon one's life.

As a child my self-awareness was non-existent. I only focused upon areas of interest to myself and was unaware of others, unless my own needs were at risk of going unnoticed. As I grew older this slowly changed. I became aware of other people, but viewed them as a nuisance. They seemed intent on interrupting me or being cross with me for not conforming to their ideas of what I should or should not be doing. It has taken me a very long time to appreciate other people's ideas about behaviour and what is understood as expected or typical, or thought of as normal. For example, it is usual to wave back to someone who waves to you. It is usual to say 'Hi' to someone who says 'Hi' to you. It seems most people don't think of this as an interruption so much as just good manners.

Now, as an adult, I have more understanding of other people. I still do not easily seek out their company but can accept that they may have a purpose in being and they are entitled to opinions that differ from mine. I also appreciate that they might mean well when they speak to me or when they phone or call over, even if they don't have an appointment. Apparently this is usual and typical of lots of people. I am learning to smile and be polite, but also to say if I don't have the time to stop and chat.

My attachments were typical and considered normal, but were they reciprocal? Did I learn from my parents and peers? I learnt some things, but they tended to refer only to my areas of interest. Schaffer (1996) cited in Wood, Littleton and Oates (2002), argues that relationships with older siblings may contain both complementary and reciprocal interactions; I conclude this can only happen if the child is aware of 'Other' and of the interaction between them. I needed others to join me at my point of interest in order for me to note theirs – for example, a family member taking the time to comment on a computer game or TV programme I was engaged in created a platform for me to look at what they might be interested in. Simply being part of the normal variation of humanity might mean some of us learn differently to others. As our difference is appreciated, valued and accommodated, learning how to stay true to oneself whilst noting how to 'fit in' with others is possible.

My brother was nine years older than me, but I remember very little about any 'place' he might have had with me as a child. This could be thought of as quite natural due to the large gap in our ages; but even though relationships within a family hierarchy offer a number of benefits that help to construct one's views and hopes for the future, common interest might be the common denominator. I think that, for me, as an autistic child, my immediate family seemed quite displaced and uninvolved in my formative years. This might be because it took longer for me to appreciate the concepts they formed more quickly than I could. However, I certainly relate well to them now. I think this is due to my being an adult and in having discovered some interests in common with them. Why wait till we grow up though? It makes so much more sense to join our interest as children and ride on the back of them to take us places we both wish to go.

Pretend play and its role as a teacher for development over the lifespan is said to be vital to the successful development of social skills and interaction with others. It is within the context of 'play' that shared meaning takes place and children begin to gain an understanding of who they are and of their role in life.

Symbolic interactionism states that the development of 'self' is interwoven with the development of a person as a social being. Of course, this may not always be a positive experience. If a child is condemned to a low place in a hierarchy with other children in their interactions (games), they may take this role on board and it could negatively influence their self-esteem. If this is so, it is even more important that we appreciate each other's differing learning styles and facilitate learning in a way that builds connection for each of us. If we only have one stamp for normal, then so many others, with so much to give, will fail to have their contributions recognized. We will be the poorer without them.

What of the effects of bullying? Will a child who is bullied by other children become a victim of others' bullying as an adult? Some do, others become the bullies in their adult lives. Dictating what is considered normal is sometimes an act of bullying. We would all benefit if we didn't allow ourselves to be bullied. The decisions we make can contribute to a society held tightly in the hands of its own life traps, or they can be part of the solution that sets us and others free.

Like so many people, women in particular, I allowed others to use and abuse me. This meant I learned my only role in life was to be there for someone else to hurt and attack. For most of my young adult life I believed this. A turning point came when I chose to stand up for myself and fight back. Why did I make that choice? What was there in my environment that enabled me to make that decision? I think it was that one other person believed in me and fought for me. Their example showed me what was possible. So maybe, as we begin to question what life is about and what we want from life and take steps to make that possible, we can begin to affect our environment as well as it affecting us.

The role of vertical relationships (parents) as well as horizontal ones (peers) seems to be obvious, but there is still some debate about it. Are children only the product of their parenting style, or do they contribute to adult outcomes by their own decisions? Most of us would say that our adult lives are the fruit of many different influences – parents, peers, television, our own decisions and those of others. Does this mean that who I am and what I become is outside of my control? It might be, but many of us in Western society have a chance to stand up for ourselves. We have a chance to challenge the status quo and a chance to make a difference, for the better, to so many other lives. Don't let this chance slip away.

As children, deciding who to listen to and what is right for us can be easy – we listen to those in authority over us. Now, as grownups, we can be that authority.

Developing without limitations

With the above in mind, and considering the explanations offered by developmental psychology concerning 'normal' development throughout the lifespan, one can see that individual experiences are so varied. Evolutionary theory has some attractive ideas, and it is obvious that concepts of normality have changed or evolved with time. Even genetics and the concepts of human development throwing out the weakest links in any chain proposes, with our changing technologies, that the larger brain and the more academic amongst us are our future. However, I suggest that all of these reasons for the development of 'normal' are too narrow and fail to take into account the broader conceptions of what is normal behaviour and normal development.

It is tempting to think that human development is a given. For example, research has shown that attachment to parents (or primary carers) in childhood is fundamental to a child's sense of wellbeing (Bowlby 1988). It also seems to figure greatly in how one's partnerships in life fare (Hazen and Shaver 1987). Then again, one could argue that even though some children have difficult childhoods, despite poor attachments to parents, they still choose to move on with their lives and 'make the most of it' (Rutter, Quinton and Hill 1990). Is this because they have fixed personality traits that dispose them towards being strong and determined? Is there a type of character, which we are either born with or not, that predetermines the fact that we will become leaders and will succeed in life? This might be one part of the equation but it isn't the whole picture. To use innate characteristics as a reason to escape responsibility for one's own life choices is a very poor excuse and doesn't hold water!

Children go through stages of cognitive development (Piaget 1954). One's own experiences bear witness to this fact, but it's also clear that each person is an individual and that this development isn't the same for everyone. Children are very literal during their formative years, probably until they are about 11 or so. After this time they become more confident in asking questions rather than just accepting what they are told, and in this way they begin to understand more abstract concepts. We would probably agree that cognitive development is a product of one's interaction with the environment. But, we no longer see development as being fixed by 'nature'.

According to Björne (2007) aspects of behaviour previously considered as innate (normal) might not be innate so much as subject to opportunity, the environment, situation and learned responses. She described an ingenious experiment with newly hatched chickens, which are known immediately to pick at and eat mealworms, showing that this is not after all an innate behaviour completely independent of experience:

> ...the newly hatched chicken were clad in taffeta socks (the rationale behind some experiments is admittedly somewhat opaque). Instead of picking at and eating the mealworms, they stared at them. If the socks were left on for two days, the chickens failed to develop normal feeding habits. The conclusion is that chickens need the experience of seeing their own toes in order for them to learn to identify mealworms as something to be eaten. Moreover, it is the experience of their own toes that is part of the development of the behavior. Toes of hens and other chickens do not suffice. (Björne 2007, p.28)

Darwin believed in 'the survival of the fittest'. In many respects I believe he is right. However, is this a biological 'given' or can we choose to become 'strong'? Maybe both concepts are true. I know that I chose 'life' and decided to fight for the right to be who I am. I could have chosen to give in to the difficulties of my life and give up. But, I didn't. This is one reason why it is important to avoid characterizing autism in terms of deficits and always to be thinking about finding a 'cure'. If there were such a cure, we might be heading towards a future without artists, computer programmers, space scientists, professors, engineers, librarians...and some writers!

Bronfenbrenner (1993) states that we each interact with our environment. We are each part of a microsystem that consists of social, symbolic and physical relationships. On a wider scale we are all part of a macrosystem that is linked by an exosystem, which is culturally and socially specific. This means that as well as us being given to a biological disposition, how the environment acts upon us and what we do with that are all contributing factors to who we are as adults.

I believe that even our thinking about development across the lifespan and how we become who we are has evolved. The new approaches to learning and positive research into exploring human development via different modalities has opened corridors into understanding that were previously lacking. We need to have an open mind and to leave dogma behind. Research needs to continue to explore and see the potential for further understanding. Genetic and biological science can be too narrow in its conception of possibilities, just as 'nurture' theorists can be. We need to understand the importance of both and make the most of appropriate healthy and adaptable environments that cater for the importance of every individual and their potential.

Unfortunately for some, typical development has evolved into a far too narrow a concept that is failing to be inclusive. We might pride ourselves in thinking we are more open-minded in the 21st century, more inclusive and more civilized than our predecessors. However, this is a myth. The very opposite has become true in so many people's experience. We sing songs of acceptance, of welcome and of the importance of belonging. But, these songs are echoes of empty wells that hold no water. They offer to quench our thirst whilst making us more thirsty!

So, if we each are the product of a mixture of biology, environmental factors, education, family values and our own decisions, how can we know who we are and exist with integrity as ourselves? What can we do to build our confidence and self-esteem? I think step 1 needs to be a place of acceptance. Rather than wishing I were someone else or that my autism or typical disposition were different, I need to say firmly to myself: 'Wendy, this is you and this is what you think, feel, believe, enjoy, desire, need, want and have.' It doesn't mean I am stuck at this point and can't change in any of these areas, but it's simply a starting place. A friend once told me that it's only when a car is in gear and the engine is running that the car can be steered in any direction. If I wait for the car to take me somewhere but the engine isn't turned on and I'm not in gear, then no matter how far down my foot goes on the gas pedal I won't be going anywhere!

After stating firmly to myself that I exist, am valuable and worthy of believing in my own potential I can set the scene for step 2.

There are things about being on the typical spectrum that can place limitations and hurdles upon one's development. The same is true for the autistic spectrum. Being typical might mean an over-sensitive awareness of what others think about you. This could lead to a preoccupation with appearance, body size, fashion and status.

Most individuals, whether typical or autistic, probably start their days with familiar routines. Why do we do this? It's because we each have been taught that this is usual/normal practice. It's usual/normal to get up after sleeping. It's usual/normal to have something to drink and eat, or simply to get washed and dressed. Maybe we do these things because we want to. I look forward to my first cup of coffee in the morning. I also look forward to breakfast. But, some individuals skip breakfast. It's just not usual for them at all. They feel more like eating or drinking after they have been up for a while.

Passing for normal is a dedicated pastime that takes up lots of time for most individuals, it's just they are so practised at it they hardly notice they are doing it. It seems we only notice when we are not practising at being our usual typical selves. For example, if I decide to walk to the local shop to buy some milk I might wear my slippers. It's not usual to go outside the house in slippers, and others might notice that I'm not wearing my shoes. It probably won't cause any great stir, but if I wore a nightgown as well, then I might be in trouble! So, even though I might not feel like getting dressed to go across the road to the shop, I probably will get dressed because it's the expected, typical and usual thing to do. Therefore, it could be argued that much of what is considered typical and normal behaviour is constructed by individuals to create order, fulfil expectations and have a set of rules that allow for minimal confusion and maximum cooperation with those rules. The difficulty occurs when the rules are broken, not adhered to or not appreciated.

I can imagine that many travellers from different countries and different cultures would have some difficulties entering a country and culture that didn't emulate their own. No wonder so many people feel on their guard all of the time to try to fit in and not upset others. The stress of such conformity must be huge!

Jacey Eckhart wrote the following short piece, which was first published in *The Virginian-Pilot* on 25 September 2007 (reprinted with the newspaper's permission).

So, how many of us really are normal anyway?

I hesitated over the box on the activity.com web site. I'd filled in all the bits required to enable a 5-year-old to play soccer. His name. His birthday. My credit card number. Then came the blank box: Is there anything else we should know about your child...

I knew this was where I was supposed to mention that Peter has autism. The league wasn't going to discriminate against Peter. These nice people wanted to carefully plan around my son's special needs. That was the problem. Peter has been doing so well at school and with his therapists that I wasn't sure he had 'special needs' when it came to playing soccer. In fact, his teacher told me that Peter would probably pass for normal someday.

'Pass' for normal. She wasn't saying Peter would be normal. Or typical. Special education teachers almost always refer to the other kind of kid as typical. My son would simply pass for normal.

That should have been good news. But something about the way she said it made me think of a section in my American history book that talked about how some light-skinned blacks once had to pass for white to get better jobs and better pay. That made me uneasy, but I clicked the send button without filling the box.

I regretted it almost from the first practice. Something about soccer seemed to make Peter act like he had every special need in the book. Sure, he chased down the ball with the other boys, but he wouldn't take off his red baseball cap because he thought he was in a Mario video game. He cried and kicked when he had to leave the field. He whined on the sidelines that he wanted to go home and put on his Halloween costume.

Last Saturday I was thinking up ways we could slink away from soccer forever, when Peter's therapist, Allison, ran up. 'Isn't he doing great? Isn't this awesome????' 'No, this is not great,' I groaned. 'This is a mistake. Why are we doing this?' Allison looked puzzled. 'Jacey, he's fine. Look at these kids. That one over there thinks he's a Power Ranger. Face it, Peter is passing for normal.' 'Passing' for normal. There it was again. But it didn't seem to me he was passing for normal. It looked to me like he was failing at being normal.

When Allison ran to coach Peter, I sank to the grass. Took a breath. Tried to see what Allison could see. I let my eye drift from my boy and onto the other people on the field. The kid who wouldn't wear socks with his cleats and shin guards. The boy on the other team who belted his own teammate when he stole the ball. Allison dodging the ball and high-fiving every kid in sight. The coach who

> knew just what to say to his kids. The young mom and dad muttering an argument about whose turn it was. The grandma plucking at the skin on her arm and pretending not to be watching the fight. Me, hiding the fact that I had a hotdog bun drenched in ketchup in my bag instead of the required orange sections all the other moms had.
>
> The whole thing was enough to make me think we are all 'passing' for normal. We are always so certain everyone else is standing exactly on the middle of normal and that we are the only ones outside the standard deviation. That can't be true. Normal is that microthin line in the exact middle of the bell curve. Only a few people stand upon it. The rest of us are like Peter standing on one side or the other and spending most of our time just trying to pass for normal.
>
> By the end of the game I'd collected enough data that I wanted to go back to that blank box. Is there anything else we should know about your child...
>
> Yeah. You should know that he's 5 and he wants to wear a soccer uniform and kick a ball in the goal. And he is passing for normal. Just like everybody else.

I really appreciate Jacey's story and her wisdom. It would be great if we all took up her reasoning and just got on with the stuff of being human. Acceptance of self whilst maintaining one's integrity could set a new standard in the concept of 'passing for normal'. Why do we continue to pretend? By not owning who we each are and not being true to self we are actually keeping up the farce, the pretence that perpetuates the lie. Let's not do this any more. If we challenge the status quo and choose not to 'blend in' but, with respect and dignity, have the courage to be who we are, then maybe we could be involved in saving the human race from one of its worst enemies – itself.

APPENDIX 1

Normal Emotions

Annoyed

Happy

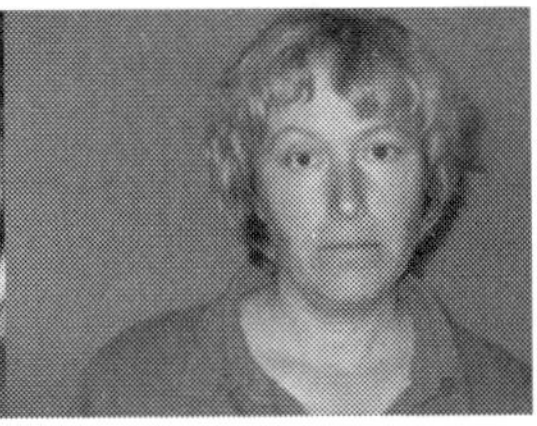
Not interested

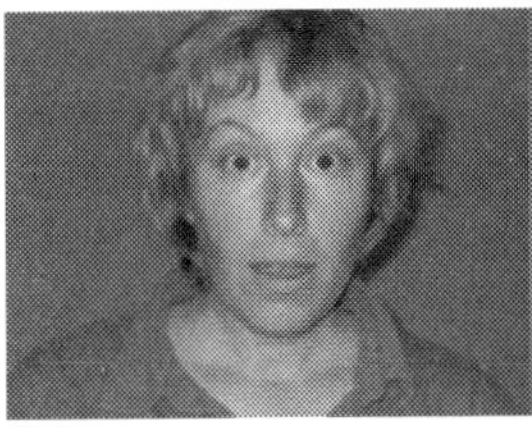
Surprised

Cross

Angry

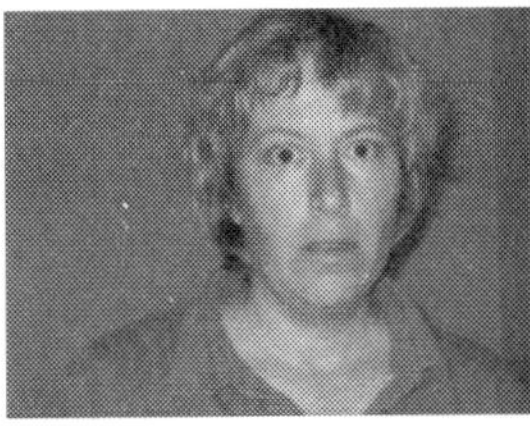
Alarmed

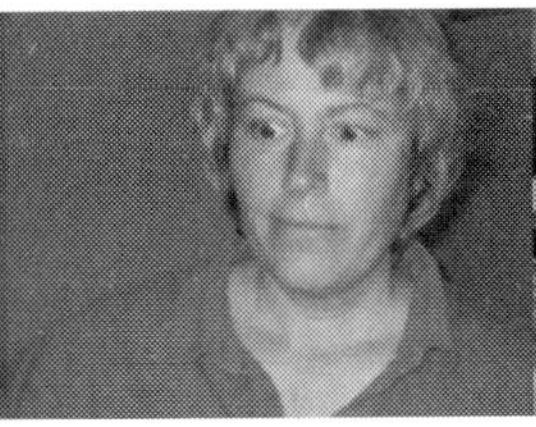
Disbelief

Sad

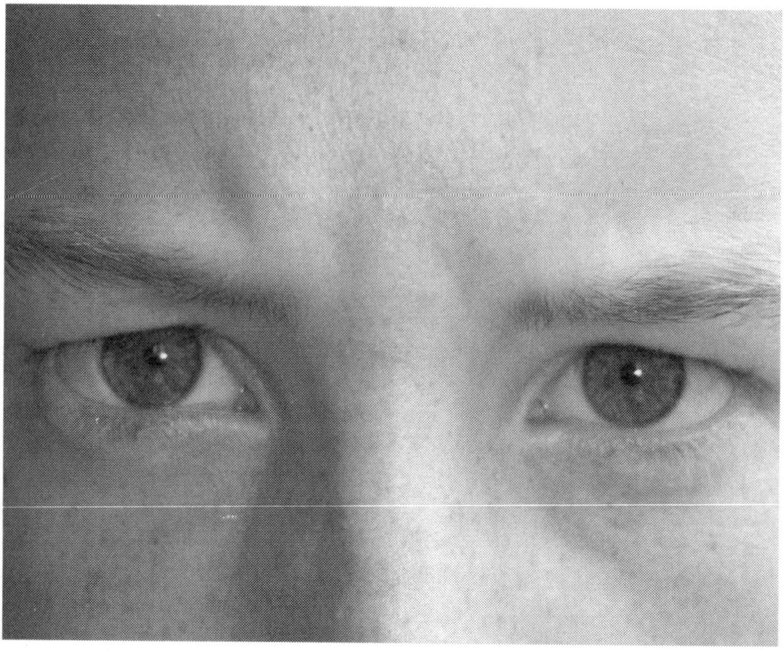

Fearful, anxious, worried

We all feel these, typical or autistic

APPENDIX 2

Hopes and Dreams

Hopes

I hope to grow up.
I hope to be well, healthy and cope.
I hope to find a friend.
I hope my partnership won't end.
I hope to get a job.
I hope to be listened to.
I hope someone will love me.
I hope I can find someone to love.
I hope school will be safe today.
I hope the bully is far away.
I hope I can last to see the day out.
I hope they hear me.
I hope I won't need to shout.
I hope I have food.
I hope he's not rude.
I hope the traffic won't be heavy.
I hope the bus will be on time.
I hope I can now get on line.
I hope the trouble moved away.
I hope my neighbours will be fine.
I hope she'll come for Christmas this year.
I hope we all get to live without fear.

Dreams

You come to me during times of sleep
and offer things just out of reach.
But I can learn to fly with birds,
to run with herds and sit with seals.
You see, in all my dreams and private thoughts
I can, I can, I can, I can.

The sun may rise, the sun may set.
The days stay long or shorter get.
It matters not, what Life will bring.
We have our dreams and hear them sing.

I am alive, I do belong.
Tomorrow is here, but not for long.
Let's make each day special; let's share our heart's dreams.
Our garments hang better when sewn at the seams.
Dreams are important, they give us each hope.
Without them our lives seem much harder to cope.
We each need each other, that's how it should be.
I need to know you and you need to know me.

References

American Psychiatric Association (1994) *Diagnostic and Statistical Manual of Mental Disorders* (4th edn Text Revision). Washington, DC: American Psychiatric Association.

Attwood, T. (1992) 'Managing the unusual behaviour of children and adults with autism.' *Communication 26*, 2, 10–11.

Attwood, T. (1998) *Asperger's Syndrome: A Guide for Parents and Professionals.* London: Jessica Kingsley Publishers.

Attwood, T. (2006) *The Complete Guide to Asperger's Syndrome.* London: Jessica Kingsley Publishers.

Autism Society Canada (2004) *Canadian Autism Research Agenda and Canadian Autism Strategy: A White Paper.* Ottawa: Autism Society Canada.

Autism Speaks (2006) 'Wrights discuss autism research with Nobel Laureate.' Available at www.autismspeaks.org/inthe news/wrights_cold_spring_harbor.php, accessed on 28 November 2007.

Baggs, A.M. (2006a) 'How many of our staff harbor scary viewpoints?' Ballastexistenz online blog. Available at http://ballastexistenz.autistics.org/?p=167, accessed on 9 February 2008.

Baggs, A.M. (2006b) 'In My Language.' YouTube online video. Available at www.youtube.com/watch?v=JnylM1hI2jc, accessed on 9 February 2008.

Baggs, A.M. (2006c) 'Learning communication skills from autistic people.' Ballastexistenz online blog. Available at http://ballastexistenz.autistics.org/?p=239, accessed on 9 February 2008.

Baird, G., Smirnoff, E., Pickles, A., Chandler, S, *et al.* (2006) 'Prevalence of disorders of the autism spectrum in a population cohort of children in South Thames: the Special Needs and Autism Project (SNAP).' *The Lancet, 368*, 210–215.

Baron-Cohen, S. (2003) *The Essential Difference: The Truth About the Male and Female Brain.* New York: Basic Books.

Baron-Cohen, S. (2005) 'The Empathizing System: A revision of the 1994 model of the mindreading system.' In B. Ellis and D. Bjorklund (eds) *Origins of the Social Mind.* New York: Guilford.

Baron-Cohen, S., Scott, F. and Stott, C. (2007) *1 in 58 Children will be Somewhere on the Autistic Spectrum.* Unpublished study. Autism Research Centre (ARC), Cambridge University.

Bauer, P.E. (2007) 'Stand tall.' Available at www.patriciaebauer.com/2007/08/23/stand-tall, accessed on 17 February 2008.

Björne, P. (2007) *A Possible World: Autism from Practice to Theory.* Lund, Sweden: Lund University Publication.

Bogdashina, O. (2003) *Sensory Perceptual Issues in Autism and Asperger Syndrome.* London: Jessica Kingsley Publishers.

Bowlby, J. (1988) *A Secure Base: Parent–Child Attachment and Healthy Human Development.* New York: Basic Books.

Bronfenbrenner, U. (1993) 'The ecology of cognitive development: Research models and fugitive findings.' In R.H. Woznick and K.W. Fischer (eds) *Development in Context.* Hillsdale, NJ: Erlbaum.

Burger, J.M. (1993) *Personality* (3rd edn). Pacific Grove, CA: Brooks/Cole.

Carter, A.S., Black, D.O., Tewani, S., Connolly, C.S., Kadlec, M.B. and Tager-Flusberg, H. (2007) 'Sex differences in toddlers with autism spectrum disorders.' *Journal of Autism and Developmental Disorders 37,* 86–97.

Centers for Disease Control and Prevention (2006, 3 March) 'Deaths associated with hypocalcemia from chelation therapy – Texas, Pennsylvania, and Oregon, 2003–2005.' *Morbidity and Mortality Weekly Report.*

Christie, J. and Enz, B.J. (1993) 'Providing resources for play.' *Childhood Education 69.*

Collier, R. (2007, 29 September) 'The politics of autism.' *The Ottawa Citizen.*

Collins, P. (2004) *Not Even Wrong: Adventures in Autism.* New York: Bloomsbury.

Cooper, T. and Roth, I. (2002) *Challenging Psychological Issues.* Milton Keynes: Open University Press.

Davis, L.J. (1997) *The Disability Studies Reader.* New York: Routledge.

Dawson, M., Soulières, I., Gernsbacher, M.A. and Mottron, L. (2007) 'The level and nature of autistic intelligence.' *Psychological Science 18,* 657–662.

Dewey, J. (1929) *The Quest for Certainty: A Study of the Relation of Knowlege and Action.* New York: Minton, Balch, and Company.

Einarsdottir, J. (2000) 'Incorporating literary resources into the play curriculum of two Icelandic preschools.' In K. Roskos and J. Christie (eds) *Play and Literacy in Early Childhood: Research from Multiple Perspectives.* Mahwah, NJ: Erlbaum.

Field, T., Field, T., Sanders, C. and Nadel, I. (2001) 'Children with autism display more social behaviors after repeated imitation sessions.' *Autism 5,* 317–323.

Freeman, S. (2003) *Science for Sale in the Autism Wars.* Langley, BC: SKF Books.

Gerland, G. (1997) *A Real Person: Life from the Outside.* Translated from the Swedish. London: Souvenir Press.

Gernsbacher, M.A., Dawson, M. and Goldsmith, H.H. (2005) 'Three reasons not to believe in an autism epidemic.' *Current Directions in Psychological Science 14,* 2, 55–58.

Ghaziuddin, M. (2005) *Mental Health Aspects of Autism and Asperger Syndrome.* London: Jessica Kingsley Publishers.

Gillberg, C. and Wing, L. (1999) 'Autism: Not an extremely rare disorder.' *Acta Psychiatr Scand 99,* 6, 399–406.

Gould, S.J. (1996) *The Mismeasure of Man.* New York: W.W. Norton & Co.

Grandin, T. (1995) 'How people with autism think.' In E. Schopler and G. Mesibov (eds) *Learning and Cognition in Autism.* New York: Plenum.

Grandin, T. (1996) *Thinking in Pictures and Other Reports from My Life with Autism.* New York: Vintage Books.

Grinker, R.R. (2007) *Unstrange Minds: Remapping the World of Autism.* New York: Basic Books.

Happé, F. and Frith, U. (2006) 'The weak coherence account: Detail focused cognitive style in autism spectrum disorders.' *Journal of Autism and Developmental Disorders 36,* 1, 5–25.

Hazen, C. and Shaver, P. (1987) 'Romantic love conceptualised as an attachment process.' *Journal of Personality and Social Psychology 52,* 3, 511–524.

Hockett, C.F. and Ascher, R. (1992) 'Inquiry and debate in the human sciences: Contributions from current anthropology, 1960–1990.' *Current Anthropology 33,* 1, 7–45.

Howlin, P. (2003) 'Outcome in high functioning adults with autism with and without early language delays: Implications for the differentiation between autism and Asperger syndrome.' *Journal of Autism and Developmental Disorders 33,* 3–13.

Interactive Autism Network (2007) 'Seeking answers: Trying anything and everything.' Available at www.iancommunity.org/cs/therapies_treatments/parents_trying_everything, accessed on 17 February 2008.

Jordan, R. (2006) 'Autism Spectrum Disorder (ASD) or Autism Spectrum Condition (ASC)?' World Autism Congress, Cape Town, South Africa.

Jordan, R.R. (2007) 'International conceptualisations, theories and treatments: New and valuable?' Available at www.awares.org/conferences, accessed 1 December 2007.

Kanner, L. (1943) 'Autistic disturbances of affective contact.' *Nervous Child 2,* 217–250.

Kanner, L. (1971) 'Follow-up study of eleven autistic children originally reported in 1943.' *Journal of Autism and Childhood Schizophrenia 1,* 2, 119–145.

King, G.A., Zwaigenbaum, L., King, S., Baxter, D., Rosenbaum, P. and Bates, A. (2006) 'A qualitative investigation of the changes in the belief systems of families of children with autism or Down syndrome.' *Child: Care, Health and Development 32,* 3, 353–369.

Kluth, C. (2003) *You're Going to Love This Kid.* Baltimore, MD: Paul Brookes.

Kunc, N. and Van Der Klift, E. (1994) 'Hell bent on helping: Benevolence, friendship and the politics of help.' In J. Thousand, R. Villa and A. Nevin (eds) *Creativity and Collaborative Learning: A Practical Guide to Empowering Students and Teachers.* Baltimore, MD: Paul Brookes.

Lawson, W. (2000) *Life Behind Glass.* London: Jessica Kingsley Publishers.

Lawson, W. (2001) *Understanding and Working with the Spectrum of Autism: An Insider's View.* London: Jessica Kingsley Publishers.

Lawson, W. (2006) *Friendships the Aspie Way.* London: Jessica Kingsley Publishers.

Lawson, W. (2007) *ASPoetry: Illustrations from an Aspie Life.* London: Jessica Kingsley Publishers.

Leary, M.R. and Baumeister, R.F. (2000) 'The nature and function of self-esteem: Sociometer theory.' In M.P. Zanna (ed.) *Advances in Experimental Social Psychology* (Vol. 32, pp.1–62). San Diego, CA: Academic Press.

Lesser, M. and Murray, D.K.C. (1998) 'Mind as a dynamical system: Implications for autism.' In *Psychobiology of Autism: Current Research and Practice.* Durham conference papers obtainable from Autism Research Unit, School of Health Sciences, University of Sunderland.

Lewis, M., Sullivan, M.W., Stanger, C. and Weiss, M. (1989) 'Self-development and self-conscious emotions.' *Child Development 60*, 1, 146–156.

Mahoney, G. and Powell, A. (1988) 'Modifying parent–child interaction: Enhancing the development of handicapped children.' *Journal of Special Education, 22*, 82–96.

Manjiviona, J. and Prior, M. (1995) 'Comparison of Asperger syndrome and high-functioning autistic children on a test of motor impairment.' *Journal of Autism and Developmental Disorders 25*, 23–39.

Marano, H.E. (2005) 'The New Sex Scorecard: Men and women's minds really do work differently – but not on everything.' Available at http://psychologytoday.com/articles/index.php?term=pto-20030624-000003, accessed on 18 May 2008.

Merchant, S. (2006) 'Learn to play and important markers in pretend play development for children with autism.' Unpublished honours thesis. Schoolf of Health and Social Development, Deakin University.

Mick, H. (2007, 13 June) 'Autism is no laughing matter.' *Globe and Mail.*

Mitchell, D.G.V., Nakic, M., Fridberg, D., Kamel, N., Pine, D.S. and Blair, R.J.R. (2007) 'The impact of processing load on emotion.' *Neuroimage 34*, 3, 1299–1309.

Mottron, L., Dawson, M., Berthiaume, C., and Soulières, I. (2004) *Peaks of ability reflect G factor in individuals with autism.* Presentation at the IMFAR conference, May. Sacramento, CA.

Mottron, L., Dawson, M., Bertone, A., and Wang, L. (2007) 'Cognitive versatility in autism cannot be reduced to a deficit.' *Cognitive Neuropsychology, 24*, 578–580.

Mottron, L., Dawson, M., Soulières, I., Hubert, B. and Burack, J.A. (2006) 'Enhanced perceptual functioning in autism: An update, and eight principles of autistic perception.' *Journal of Autism and Developmental Disorders 36*, 27–43.

Murray, D.K.C. (1986) *Language and Interests.* PhD thesis, University of London.

Murray, D.K.C. (1992) 'Attention tunnelling and autism.' In P. Shattock and G. Linfoot (eds) *Living with Autism: The Individual, the Family and the Professional.* Sunderland: Autism Research Unit, School of Health Sciences, University of Sunderland.

Murray, D.K.C. (2000) *Wrong Planet Syndrome.* Available at www.autismusundcomputer.de/wrongplanetsyndrom.en.html, accessed on 10 February 2008.

Murray, D.K.C., Lesser, M. and Lawson, W. (2005) 'Attention, monotropism and the diagnostic criteria for autism.' *International Journal of Research and Practice: Autism 9*, 2, 139–156.

Murray, D. and Lawson, W. (2007) 'Inclusion through technology for autistic children.' In Ruth Cigman (ed.) *Included or Excluded: The Challenge of the Mainstream for Some SEN Children.* London: Routledge.

NAS (National Autistic Society) (2007) *Thinking Differently Campaign.* London: Channel 4.

Neuman, S. and Roskos, K. (1992) 'Literary objects as cultural tools: Effects on children's literacy behaviors.' *Reading Research Quarterly 27*, 3, 202–225.

Nietzsche, F. (1974) The Gay Science: With a Prelude in Rhymes and an Appendix of Songs. New York: Vintage Books.

Peterson, C. (1989) *Looking Forward Through the Lifespan.* London: Prentice Hall.

Piaget, P. (1954) *The Construction of Reality in a Child.* New York: Basic Books.

Piers, M. and Landau, G. (1980) *The Gift of Play and Why Children Cannot Thrive Without It.* New York: Walker and Company.

Plutchik, R. (1962) *The Emotions: Facts, Theories and a New Model.* New York: Random House.

Plutchik, R. (1982) 'A psychoevolutionary theory of emotions.' *Social Science Information 21*, 529–553.

Prior, M.R. (2003) *Learning and Behavioral Problems in Asperger's Syndrome.* New York: Guilford Press.

Rickarby, G., Carruthers, A. and Mitchell, M. (1991) 'Brief report: Biological factors associated with Asperger Syndrome.' *Journal of Autism and Developmental Disorders 21*, 3, 341–392.

Russ, S. (1993) *Affect and Creativity: The Role of Affect and Play in the Creative Process.* Hillsdale, NJ: Erlbaum.

Rutherford, M.D., Richards, E.D., Moldes, V. and Sekuler, A.B. (2007) 'Evidence of a divided-attention advantage in autism.' *Cognitive Neuropsychology 24*, 5, 505–515.

Rutter, M., Quinton, D. and Hill, J. (1990) 'Adult outcome of institution-reared children: Males and females compared.' In L.N. Robins and M. Rutter (eds) *Straight and Devious Pathways from Childhood to Adulthood.* Cambridge: Cambridge University Press.

Ryokai, K., Vaucelle, C. and Cassell J. (2003) 'Virtual peers as partners in storytelling and literacy learning.' *Journal of Computer Assisted Learning, 19*, 195–208.

Savarese, R. J. (2007) *Reasonable People: A Memoir of Autism and Adoptio*n. New York: Other Press.

Seach, D. (2007) *Interactive Play for Children with Autism.* London: Routledge.

Segar, M. (1997) *Coping – A Survival Guide for People with Asperger Syndrome.* Nottingham: Early Years Diagnostic Centre. (Also avalable online at www.autismandcomputing.org.uk/marc2en.html, accessed on 28 November 2007).

Seidel, K. (2005) 'Evidence of venom: An open letter to David Kirby, author, Evidence of Harm.' Available at www.neurodiversity.com/evidence_of_venom.html, accessed on 17 February 2008.

Shalom, D.B., Mostofsky, S.H., Hazlett, R.L., Goldberg, M.C. *et al.* (2006) 'Normal physiological emotions but differences in expression of conscious feelings in children with high-functioning autism.' *Journal of Autism and Developmental Disorders 35*, 3, 395–400.

Sharpley, C., Bitsika, V. and Efremidis, B. (1997) 'The influence of gender, parental health, and perceived expertise of assistance upon the well-being of parents of children with autism.' *Journal of Intellectual and Developmental Disability 22*, 1, 19–28.

Sinclair, J. (1987) 'Intersexuality.' Available at http://web.syr.edu/~jisinla/index.html, accessed on 18 May 2008.

Sinclair, J. (1993) 'Don't mourn for us.' *Our Voice: Autism Network International Newsletter 1*, 3. Also available online at http://ani.autistics.org/dont_mourn.html, accessed on 9 February 2008.

Sinclair, J. (1998) 'Concerns about inclusion from within the disability community.' Available at http://web.syr.edu/~jisincla/inclusion.htm, accessed on 22 February 2008.

Smith, J. (2007) *Murder of Autistics.* Available at http://thiswayoflife.org/murder.html, accessed on 9 February 2008.

Stone, S.J. and Christie, J.F. (1996) 'Collaborative literacy learning during sociodramatic play in a multiage (K-2) primary classroom.' *Journal of Research in Childhood Education 10*, 2, 123–133.

Taubes, G. (2007, 16 September) 'What really makes us healthy.' *New York Times Magazine.*

Tavris, C. (1992) *The Mismeasure of Woman.* New York: Simon and Schuster.

Thierry, L. and Solomon, E. (2006) *Autism Every Day* [Film]. Available at www.autismspeaks.org/sponsoredevents/autism_every_day.php, accessed on 9 February 2008.

Wady, P. and Culling, E. (2007) 'I describe myself as being emotionally flat.' YouTube online video. Available at www.youtube.com/watch?v=6dRBLYUWxyI, accessed on 9 February 2008.

Waterhouse, S. (2000) *A Positive Approach to Autism.* London: Jessica Kingsley Publishers.

Williams, D. (1994) *Somebody Somewhere.* London: Jessica Kingsley Publishers.

Wing, L. (1988) 'The continuum of autistic characteristics.' In E. Schopler and G.B. Mesibov (eds) *Diagnosis and Assessment in Autism.* New York: Plenum.

Wing, L. (1992) 'Manifestations of social problems in high-functioning autistic people.' In E. Schopler and G.B. Mesibov (eds) *High Functioning Individuals with Autism.* New York: Plenum.

Wood, C., Littleton, K. and Oates, J. (2002) 'Lifespan development.' In T. Cooper and I. Roth (eds) *Challenging Psychological Issues.* Milton Keynes: Open University Press.

Young, J.E. and Klosko, J.S. (1994) *Reinventing Your Life: How to Break Free from Negative Life Patterns.* New York: Plume Books.

Useful Resources

About using technology

Murray, D.K.C. and Aspinall, A. (2005) *Getting IT.* London: Jessica Kingsley Publishers.

About social skills acquisition

Edmonds, G. and Beardon, L. (eds) (2008) *Asperger Syndrome and Social Relationships: Adults Speak Out About Asperger Syndrome.* London: Jessica Kingsley Publishers.

Hesmondhalgh, M. and Breakey, C. (2001) *Access and Inclusion for Children with Autistic Spectrum Disorders: 'Let Me In'.* London: Jessica Kingsley Publishers.

Lawson, W. (2003) *Build Your Own Life.* London: Jessica Kingsley Publishers.

Lawson, W. (2004) *Sex, Sexuality and the Autism Spectrum.* London: Jessica Kingsley Publishers.

About our 'normality'

Hoopmann, K. (2006) *All Cats Have Asperger Syndrome.* London: Jessica Kingsley Publishers.

Hoy, R. (2007) *Autism and Me* (DVD). London: Jessica Kingsley Publishers.

Lawson, W. (2006) *ASPoetry: Illustrated Poems from an Aspie Life.* London: Jessica Kingsley Publishers.

Murray, D.K.C. (ed.) (2005) *Coming out Asperger: Diagnosis, Disclosure and Self-confidence.* London: Jessica Kingsley Publishers.

Web pages

Neurodiversity: http://neurodiversity.com

'Personal Definitions of Sexuality' by Jim Sinclair: http://web.syr.edu/%7Ejisincla/definitions.htm

Sexuality and disability resources: www.farnorthernrc.org/mylifemychoice/Books.htm

Wendy Lawson's web page: www.mugsy.org/wendy

Subject Index

Author Index